ED VS. YUMMY FUR

Or, What Happens When a Serial Comic
Becomes a Graphic Novel

Other Books In The Critical Cartoons Series:

Carl Barks' Duck by Peter Schilling Jr.

Ed vs. Yummy Fur: Or, What Happens When a Serial Comic Becomes a Graphic Novel
Critical Cartoons 001

Copyright © 2014 Brian Evenson & Uncivilized Books.

Yummy Fur and *Ed the Happy Clown* artwork is reproduced by permission and is
copyright © Chester Brown.

Series Editor/Designer: Tom Kaczynski
Production assistants: Joel McKeen & Kathleen Berry.

Uncivilized Books
P.O. Box 6434
Minneapolis, MN 55406
USA

uncivilizedbooks.com

First Edition, May 2014
10 9 8 7 6 5 4 3 2 1

ISBN 978-0-9846814-9-5

DISTRIBUTED TO THE TRADE BY:

Consortium Book Sales & Distribution, LLC.
34 Thirteenth Avenue NE,
Suite 101 Minneapolis,
MN 55413-1007
Orders: (800) 283-3572

Printed in the USA

ED VS. YUMMY FUR

Or, What Happens When a Serial Comic Becomes a Graphic Novel

....

by Brian Evenson

Uncivilized Books

CONTENTS

INTRODUCTION

The idea for this book started just a few days after Drawn & Quarterly's 2012 re-release of *Ed the Happy Clown*. More specifically, it started when I picked up that book in the bookstore and noticed the subtitle: "*a graphic-novel*". Chester Brown's name was in all-caps, the title too was all-caps, which drew my attention to the fact that the subtitle seemed deliberately lowercase. Part of me felt this was simply just a matter of typography, a choice made to distinguish between title and subtitle. But another part of me believed—and still believes—that there are no accidents, and that it is these small, seemingly random choices that accumulate into the larger distinctions that end up shaping not only a book but an entire genre.

Standing there in Modern Times, I found myself wondering what made a 'graphic-novel' different from a 'Graphic Novel'? It seemed a question of simple arithmetic: the subtraction of capitalization and the addition of a hyphen. The first gesture strips away a level of formatting, going against common title capitalization guidelines. The second adds a piece of formatting we wouldn't expect to be there, a hyphen, and which isn't there in any other use of the phrase "graphic novel" that I can remember. Both seem incredibly small things. But it is of such small things that greater effects are both built and sustained.

Speaking of Wile E. Coyote falling off cliffs in his *Road Runner* cartoons, Chuck Jones talks about how the effectiveness of a gesture can come down to a single frame of film. "When the Coyote fell off, I knew he had to go exactly eighteen frames into the distance and then disappear for fourteen frames before he hit." "It seemed to me that thirteen frames didn't work in terms of humor, and neither did fifteen frames. Fourteen frames got a laugh."[1] So, the humor of the Coyote's landing depends on the camera staying with his disappearance exactly the right amount of time instead of letting it go $1/24^{th}$ of a second too early or $1/24^{th}$ of a second too late. $1/24^{th}$ of a second is a length of time twice as fast as what the eye can process as a separate image—it can't actually be seen as an image but only as part of a motion. But that imperceptible difference is still what the humor of Wile E. Coyote's fall depends on.

Why lowercase, then? And what does the hyphen do? Are these choices arbitrary or can they tell us something about *Ed the Happy Clown*? Can we gain anything from interrogating them closely?

lowercase

The lack of capitalization, an analyst might tell you, suggests deference, an unwillingness to insist on the term, a minimizing of its importance. You might see it as analogous to what Deleuze and Guattari call writing in a minor language: a refusal to claim the authority that a generally accepted term like "Graphic Novel" has come to have. With *Ed* having developed not independently but as part of an ongoing comic, *Yummy Fur*, the idea that it is a graphic novel can only be a kind of afterthought, and perhaps is not to be insisted upon.

Before it was a "graphic-novel", from 1983 to 1985, the first parts

....

[1] Quoted in Hugh Kenner, *Chuck Jones: A Flurry of Drawings* (Berkeley: University of California Press, 1994), 64, 47.

of *Ed* were part of a seven-issue mini-comic called *Yummy Fur*. Then from 1986 to 1989 all of *Ed*—including all the mini-comic material and Ed-related material that was to be later deliberately left out of the "graphic-novel"—was part of the first 18 issues of a 32-issue comic book series also called *Yummy Fur* (December 1986-January 1994). Then in 1989, the Ed material from the first twelve issues of the *Yummy Fur* comic book series was collected as *Ed the Happy Clown: A Yummy Fur Book*. Instead of being identified as a graphic novel, there was still a sense at this time of *Ed* and *Yummy Fur* being connected, and that connection was something to be asserted in the subtitle. That 1989 book, when it was published, was considered by Brown to be incomplete, and Brown spoke in January of 1990 of printing the rest of the *Ed* material as a second volume,[2] an idea that he quickly dropped.

Instead, in 1992 Brown brought out *Ed the Happy Clown: The Definitive Ed Book*. This is the edition that established what he felt to be the definitive narrative of the Ed story. To do so, Brown deliberately abridged the Ed story as it had appeared in *Yummy Fur*, getting rid of the majority of the Ed material from *Yummy Fur* issues 13-18, and cobbling together a new ending. All the editions of *Ed* since, whether the 2012 book or the 2005-2006 Drawn & Quarterly 9-issue reprint, stick to this abridgement and alternate ending.

You could argue that *Ed the Happy Clown: The Definitive Ed Book* is the moment that *Ed the Happy Clown* becomes a graphic novel—in 1992, nine years after the first mini-comic containing Ed was published. But it wasn't called one at that time. It doesn't get that subtitle until 2012, 29 years after Ed the Happy Clown first appeared

....

[2] From the letters pages (called by Brown the "Fur Bag") of issue #19 of *Yummy Fur*: "I only realized I was wrapping up the Ed saga while I was halfway through writing and drawing YF#17. (I think I was on page nine.) This would have been late June and the Ed book was too far into production to pull. Still we can always print a second Ed book reprinting 13-18 sometime or other. The orders for the book at hand, though, have been so ridiculously low that we're not anxious to rush into print with another one."

in Brown's comic. It's also important to remember that Ed became a graphic novel by letting go of its three successive past-lives as 1) a part of a mini-comic, 2) a part of a comic books series, and 3) a book with a different ending.[3] *Ed the Happy Clown: a graphic-novel* is a very late incarnation of Ed. What was stripped away with each incarnation is as important in establishing what Ed was and now is as what remains.

LINKAGES

As Brown suggested to me: "I've never been happy with the term graphic novel. It's too obviously an attempt to sound respectable. But it's caught on now, for whatever reason, so there's not much use in fighting it." And yet the way Brown writes the term on the cover of the 2012 edition, as "graphic-novel", suggests that he still has at least a little resistance and fight left in him.

Brown joins the two terms with a hyphen: "graphic-novel". That's not the way the term usually appears, and grammatically it's a little strange. Usually the term is "graphic novel" with "novel" being the main noun and "graphic" the adjective that modifies it—one term is clearly secondary to the other. That also suggests something about the prominence and importance of the one rather than the other. It's not a "novelized comic", it's a "graphic novel."[4]

....

[3] Says Brown about *Yummy Fur*, in response to Scott Grammel's question in a *Comics Journal* interview, "Where do you draw the line as to where an ongoing graphic novel ends": "…when you're doing a comic book as an ongoing series… if I had started doing this as a graphic novel—as a novel—then I would have no trouble with it. But I don't think of it first as a novel." (90). See Scott Grammel, "Interview with Chester Brown," in *The Comics Journal* 135 (April 1990), 66-90.

[4] Douglas Wolk speaks, relatedly, of the problems of using other forms or genres as modifiers for comics, objecting to the way this sometimes ends up being a valorization: "Good comics are sometimes described as being 'cinematic' or 'novelistic'.… These can be descriptive words when they're applied to comics. It's almost an insult, though, to treat them as compliments." (13) Cf. Douglas Wolk,

Phrased as "graphic-novel," however, it feels like a compound word is beginning to form, one in which each term has equal weight, equal importance. It's a step on the way to "graphicnovel" (at least it would be if we were German), where there's no longer a separation between the graphic qualities and the novelistic qualities, but each is seen as integral to the other: one word instead of two.

Of course, as a reader, when I read "graphic-novel" I know I'm basically being told something is a "graphic novel", but there's that little tick of difference, that little tick of *offness*, that I think characterizes Brown's work as a whole. To experience both *Yummy Fur* and *Ed the Happy Clown* as productively as possible, you have to be willing to think a little differently than you usually do. The hyphen in the subtitle cues that.

I mean this not only in terms of Brown's content, which is often strange and challenging—disturbing enough that it's hard to recommend *Yummy Fur* or *Ed the Happy Clown* to just anyone without offering a few caveats/qualifiers/warnings (for instance, "If you won't be offended by a comic that has a clown's penis replaced by President Reagan's head, you'll find this an amazing story"). I mean it also in terms of form. Generally, we think about comics as functioning not only as a series of panels implying a progression of time, but as a sequence of pages: the relationship of the panels on the page can be as important as the sequential relationship of the first panel to the second to the third, and so on. Brown, however, draws each panel individually. (see Fig. 1) Says Brown, "Unlike most narrative print cartoonists, I *never* think about the page as a whole when I'm drawing. I think either about the individual panel or how it will work in a scene, but never about the page because I won't know which panels will go on which pages until I'm finished with everything and I'm assembling the work for publication. I guess

Reading Comics: How Graphic Novels Work and What They Mean (Boston: Da Capo Press, 2007).

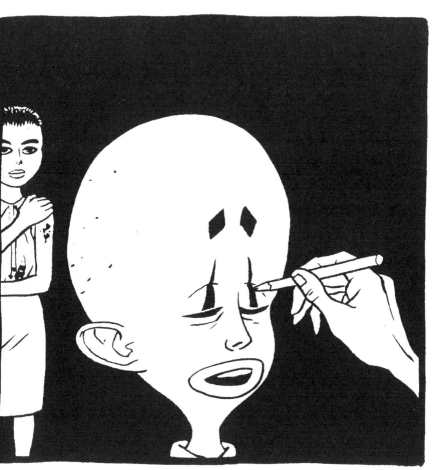

Fig. 1. Actual size Brown draws his panels. *Yummy Fur* #18, 20:1.

I think of each scene as a central unit."[5] In other words, Brown is very concerned both with the panel as a unit of meaning[6] and an entire scene as a unit of meaning, but the intermediate stage, the *pages* made up of panels that *form* the scene, is not something he considers while he is drawing. This allows him to feel that he can shift a panel's position, say, from page 3 panel 6 to page 4 panel 1 without any repercussions. Indeed, he makes many such changes between *Yummy Fur* and the 2012 *Ed* book.[7]

And yet, we as readers of comics have been trained to think of the page as important, because we've read so many comics in which it *is* important. Whatever Brown's intention, the page still remains a unit of meaning that readers can and will draw on. Shifting the panels slightly, then, will, for most readers, have an impact on the effect of the whole in the same way that that extra frame of film can make the Coyote's fall either less or more funny.

....

[5] Douglas Wolk affirms: "Brown is less concerned with the page as a visual or narrative unit than almost any other comic book artist." (152) Brown has been working this way since very early in his career, starting with "Walrus Blubber Sandwich." As he says in the notes for *The Little Man*, "Later, when I started drawing longer strips, I realized how convenient this technique is for editing a strip. Adding, removing or rearranging individual panels or whole scenes is easy when pages don't have a fixed arrangement." (162)

[6] And yet, only rarely does Brown present work in a way that isn't laid out like a traditional comics page. He does, however, in *The Playboy* and a few other pieces, offer fewer panels per pages, two or three mostly, though sometimes single-page panels as well, which perhaps allows the reader to experience the work in a way closer to how Brown draws it and thinks about it.

[7] In addition, in his notes on the 2012 *Ed* he comments on a moment when this way of working ends up being detrimental. "In creating strips this way, there is the danger that panels won't 'work' together" (221). On pages 223 he shows an example of the way that a particular juxtaposition places a panel depicting Josie's head and shoulders almost directly over a panel depicting Ed's chest, torso and legs, including the exposed Reagan-headed penis, creating a hermaphroditic exquisite corpse. Brown found this particular juxtaposition unfortunate enough that in the 2012 version of *Ed* he cropped one of the panels to shift it slightly and avoid it (see 89:1 and 89:3).

Fig. 2. *Ed the Happy Clown*, 59:2

DISTINCTION & MEANING

What I've been talking about so far are largely questions of precision, small choices that can bring the right or wrong amount of focus to bear on a story. But since they are choices, there is also a question of distinction: making one choice, whether arbitrarily or not, means that you are not making another choice. Each choice takes a path and a direction. The aggregate of choices either adds up to something like a roadmap leading the reader somewhere or makes the reader feel adrift, unsure of where he or she is heading.

Even a small choice can shift the meaning in a way that has quite a large impact. If I'm standing beside a light switch in a pitch-black room, the small choice of whether to flick it before I cross the room will have a major impact on every step of the journey thereafter (see Fig. 2).

Meaning, structuralism suggests, resides first in the phoneme, the smallest bit of meaningful sound in the language. A shift in phoneme shifts the meaning of a verbal utterance—which is why we can distinguish between the word "cat" and the word "cot" and know which one refers to something we'd prefer to sleep on. If you can't recognize the shift in phoneme, you don't recognize the shift in meaning, and you end up thinking someone is talking about one thing when in fact they're talking about another. If you come from a place where the short i in "pin" and the short e of "pen" are pronounced the same, you well may not be able to hear, or even replicate, a difference when you are around people who do pronounce "pin" and "pen" distinctly differently.[8] You're in real trouble if you can't hear the difference between "Fore!" and "Fire!"— you may duck when you should instead stop, drop, and roll. One letter shifts, one sound changes slightly, and a meaning can become something else entirely.

CHANGES

This book is not a work of bibliography. It does not intend to catalog *every* change between *Yummy Fur*'s Ed and the 2012 *Ed* edition, but it will examine different *types* of changes that occur, consider what these changes mean as Ed moves from mini-comic through comic-book series to graphic-novel, and ultimately try to give a sense of how the graphic novel differs from the *Yummy Fur* material that gave birth to it.

Those changes come in all magnitudes, ranging from the very small to the quite large. On one end of the spectrum we have a slight or large change in a panel—the redrawing of a panel, say, or a modification of it (as with the famous censored erect penis in

....

[8] Linguists call this the "pin-pen merger". If you're from the Western half or upper half of the country, chances are you pronounce "pin" and "pen" differently. If you're from the South or Southeast you probably don't, and have developed ways of making that distinction clear from context (i.e. "You mean the one you write with? Or the one you sew with?").

Yummy Fur #4 and its restoration in the 2012 *Ed*). That's followed on the spectrum by the shifting of the placement of panels on the page, for instance. That's followed in turn by massive narrative re-organization, such as the cutting of most of the material in YF#13-18 and the modification of the ending. At the far end of the spectrum is the formal/generic shift of moving from a mini-comic to a multi-issue floppy to a book. The experience of reading *Ed* changes with each shift, particularly in its distillation into a single independent story in book form, which moves it away from its quite troubling serial interaction with the gospel tales in *Yummy Fur*.

We'll look too at a few moments that make a different kind of sense in *Yummy Fur* than they do in *Ed*. For instance, we have more of a context for understanding who Christian is in *Yummy Fur* than we do in *Ed*. Same goes for Bick Backman and his family; we can only understand what might be at stake for them if we have the additional material that Brown chose to cut. Otherwise, they remain flat, minor characters.

GENRE

For me, Chester Brown's *Yummy Fur/Ed the Happy Clown* is important not only because it's a great (albeit disturbing) story drawn in interesting ways. It's important in that it is one of the few works that spans all the formal developments of independent comics (except for the latest one, the web comic). It began as a mini-comic and has ended up as a "graphic-novel", and in between was a multi-volume floppy and a multi-volume single-story re-issue. *Ed the Happy Clown* is a story that seems to have responded to these shifts in form by changing to accommodate them. As a result, looking closely at the differences between *Yummy Fur* and *Ed* is a way of reflecting on shifts in format and genre as well, thinking about how they change the story. Both form and genre are systems of organization and, thus, are systems of control. As such, they shape the way in which a story can be told. *Ed* is interesting because it starts out as one thing in one form and then becomes another thing in another. Not unlike the Ed in the *Yummy Fur* version, who ends up poorly impersonating Bick Backman, the later version of the story itself shows the marks and scars of its origins if you look closely. How we talk about something, how we define it, what we see as the ultimate end-product, determines how we see it as readers, and how we think about it as writers.

THE DEATH OF YUMMY FUR

At the time of this writing, copies of *Yummy Fur* are harder and harder to find. Those of us who first approached *Ed* through that version are reaching (or passing) middle age. The comic writers and graphic novelists who were influenced by *Yummy Fur* have gone on to influence budding comic artists themselves. It seems more and more apparent that the version of the Ed story found in the 2012 *Ed the Happy Clown* is how Ed will be remembered rather than through the version that appeared in *Yummy Fur*.[9]

The purpose of this book, ultimately, is to think about what will be gained and what will be lost as *Yummy Fur* slips out of the cultural consciousness and *Ed the Happy Clown* takes its place. To think closely about the small and large distinctions between them and the way these add up to something quite a bit larger, and quite significant. To try to understand the reason *Yummy Fur* had the impact it did, and to try to understand the way in which its ghost still haunts *Ed the Happy Clown*. And, indirectly, to think about

....

[9] Brown seems to prefer this. When I asked him, "How do you feel knowing that the *Yummy Fur* version might be lost to most readers?" he responded "Happy." There's a playfulness to this response, considering *Yummy Fur* is being replaced by something called *Ed the Happy Clown*, but it does seem to be Brown's honest opinion nonetheless.

what it means for floppy single-issue comics to have receded from prominence and for "graphic novels" (whatever that means) to have taken their place. The transition from *Yummy Fur* to *Ed the Happy Clown* marks an important transition in independent comics, and understanding what is gained and lost might well help us understand how our thinking about the field of comics has both consciously and unconsciously changed as well as predicting how it might continue to change in the future.

Fig. 3. *Ed the Happy Clown*, 31:2

CHAPTER ONE:
SCATOLOGY

One thing neither *Ed the Happy Clown* nor *Yummy Fur* have ever been accused of is being squeamish. Brown seems to have no hesitation about violating religious, sexual, and scatological taboos along the way to telling the Ed story, and indeed all these transgressions are integral to the story itself. But among the most central—considering the way a dead man's asshole provides a link between our dimension and a parallel universe and that it's this same man's inability to stop shitting that ends up breaking Ed out of prison early on—is his focus on sewage and excrement.

One of the earliest Ed-related pieces is "The Man Who Couldn't Stop". It is a simple two-page comic, twelve panels total, six panels per page. In both *Yummy Fur* and *Ed*, we don't turn the page, but have the first and second pages facing one another, allowing us to take in the whole sequence almost at a glance. Besides the title (which fills the first panel), the caption "A Public Washroom" (at the top of the second panel), and a thought bubble in the final panel, the comic is wordless. Its progression of images is fairly static as well: panels 3-12 depict the same man sitting on the toilet in more or less the same position (see Fig. 4), until we reach his final thoughts: "Hmn… can't seem to stop."

In both the *Yummy Fur* mini-comic (the seven issues of which are

Fig. 4. *Ed the Happy Clown*, 25:5

nearly exactly reproduced in the first three issues of the *Yummy Fur* comic) and the *Yummy Fur* serial comic, "The Man Who Couldn't Stop" appears as one of a number of seemingly distinct pieces. There's nothing to let us know up-front that it's connected to the Ed story.[1]

Yummy Fur the comic arranges them this way[2]:

SEQUENCE OF *YUMMY FUR*

Issue #1

1a. Cover of mini-comic YF#1: a picture of a woman on a toilet, with the toilet paper speaking to her, saying "I'm not going to take it anymore."

1. Walrus Blubber Sandwich* [3]

2. The Toilet Paper Revolt*

3a. Cover of mini-comic YF#2: a close-up from the sixth panel of "Ed the Happy Clown"

3. Ed the Happy Clown [the first Ed story, involving rats and Ed breaking his leg]

....

[1] Brown, however, indicates that "The Man Who Couldn't Stop" was never "intended as a stand-alone strip—I knew when I drew these panels that the story of the-man-who-couldn't-stop would continue." (*Ed*, 212) In the Grammel interview he adds "Well, in the case of 'The Man Who Couldn't Stop' I knew that he was going to be the character that he became in the storyline… I knew it was going to fit into that next story, the Ed the Happy Clown story, but I didn't know all about the other dimension and everything. That stuff came later." (83)

[2] Since *Yummy Fur* the comic reproduces all seven issues of the mini-comic exactly and in order, I'll only speak about the comic here. It is worth noting, though, that there are differences in format moving from mini-comic to serial comic, something I'll address later on.

[3] An asterisk (*) in this list indicates a piece that, although not included in the book *Ed the Happy Clown*, can be found in Brown's *The Little Man: Short Strips 1980-1995*.

4. Mars*

5a. Cover of the mini-comic YF#3: a close-up from a painting in the final panel of "Mars"[4]

5. Bob Crosby and His Electric T.V.*

6. City Swine*

Issue #2

7a. Cover of the mini-comic YF#4: a panel from the fourth page of "The Eyelid Burial"

7. Catlick Creek[†][5]

8. The Eyelid Burial[†]

9. Adventures in Science [masturbating squid episode]

10. Fire with Fire[†]

11a. Cover of mini-comic YF#5: a picture of Frankenstein, with Ed in the background.[6]

11. Ed and the Beanstalk

12a. Cover of mini-comic YF#6: The words "Yummy Fur" as if drawn in black chalk, with a gaunt hand in a box in the upper right hand corner.

12. Adventures in Science [image of Jesus on a piece of masking tape episode]

....

[4] Interesting that Brown offers here neither something unique nor something from the issue for which it is the cover, but something from the final image of the last issue. He uses a variation of this same image for the cover of YF#1 as well, choosing to introduce readers to the Vortex edition of the comic with an image from a story that he won't reproduce in *Ed the Happy Clown*.

[5] The symbol "†" indicates short pieces that Brown did not collect in *The Little Man* or elsewhere, and which only appear in *Yummy Fur*. More on these pieces later.

[6] This image will be used as the title page for the "Introductory Pieces" section of the *Ed* graphic novel.

13. Joke Time[†]

    Issue #3[7]

14. Joke Time[†]

15. Crime and Punishment with Ed the Happy Clown

16. Adventures in Science [piano or worm episode]

17. Garbage Day[*]

18. My Old Neighborhood[*]

19. The Man Who Couldn't Stop

20. An Authentic Inuit Folk Song[*]

21. I Live in the Bottomless Pit[*]

22. Ed the Happy Clown in Confinement

23. Adventures in Science [werewolves episode, which fades into the Ed story]

It's worth noting that for the first two issues in particular of the Vortex *Yummy Fur*, Brown seems to want to simulate the experience of reading the mini-comic, including presenting each mini-comic as separate and distinct: you know when one mini-comic stops and the next begins.[8] There's a certain amount of confusion in this, in that, for instance, *Yummy Fur* #1 contains (the mini-comics) *Yummy Fur* #1, *Yummy Fur* #2, and *Yummy Fur* #3. Since Brown preserves the mini-

....

[7] In YF#3, Brown does not reproduce the cover of mini-comic YF#7 within the comic. Instead, he uses it as the cover for the issue itself, but doesn't acknowledge having done so up front. At the end of the issue, on the inside back cover, he does reproduce it as it was in the mini-comic and explains that the issue is a combination of a couple of pieces from *Yummy Fur* (mini) #6 and #7. To me, Brown not using the cover to mark the transition from #6 to #7 within the comic is an indication that he's now thinking in terms of a comic rather than in terms of reproducing a mini-comic.

[8] With the exception of #7…

Fig. 5. *Ed the Happy Clown*, 29:5

comic covers and since the names are the same, we end up experiencing two overlapping organizational systems, one nesting within the other.

In any case, even not counting the covers, we have eighteen comics before "The Man Who Couldn't Stop", and only a few of them are either directly or indirectly Ed-related. The overall effect, for a good part of the first three Vortex *Yummy Fur* issues, is of a diffuse collection of varied pieces. It is *not* of a story building up. True, there are more Ed pieces than anything else, but they are scattered through a lot of different sorts of things. Each Vortex issue, too, averages almost eight separate very short pieces per issue.

This changes with *Yummy Fur* #4, the first issue that Brown wrote exclusively for Vortex (having run out of mini-comic material at that point). From here on out, each issue will alternate between, at most, two story lines (Ed and the gospel of Mark initially). Instead of continuing to offer a fistful of short comics, *Yummy Fur* from here on out dedicates itself to continuing multi-issue stories. Brown has begun to think in terms of longer projects.

In the 2012 graphic novel (and in all the book forms of *Ed the Happy Clown*), "The Man Who Couldn't Stop" is contextualized quite differently. It's part of a section called "Introductory Pieces" that begin the volume, which consists of a short series of pieces that originally seemed in *Yummy Fur* to be discrete and distinct. Now they are used consciously by Brown (some more directly than others) to build up the Ed story. In his introduction to *The Little Man*, Brown speaks of this: "Some of my early short strips, which were at first intended to stand complete at a few pages, were later incorporated into the long serial 'Ed the Happy Clown'" (ix).

"Introductory Pieces" is arranged as follows. I've preserved the numbering system of the *Yummy Fur* list above so it will immediately be clear to readers where the gaps and rearrangements are:

SEQUENCE OF *ED THE HAPPY CLOWN*

11a. Cover of mini-comic YF#5

3. Ed the Happy Clown [the first Ed story, involving rats and Ed breaking his leg]

9. Adventures in Science [masturbating squid episode]

11. Ed and the Beanstalk

12. Adventures in Science [image of Jesus on a piece of masking tape episode]

15. Crime and Punishment with Ed the Happy Clown

16. Adventures in Science [piano or worm episode]

19. The Man Who Couldn't Stop

22. Ed the Happy Clown in Confinement

Not counting the covers, we've gone from 22 pieces down to 8, a much more manageable number. Except for "The Man Who Couldn't Stop," the pieces that Brown retains are obviously related either to 1) "Ed the Happy Clown" or to 2) "Adventures in Science"—and indeed the first piece in chapter one of the "graphic-novel" will be the werewolves episode (see Fig. 5) of "Adventures in Science," which will weave these two story threads together and thus explain and justify the inclusion of "Adventures in Science" earlier.

In *Ed the Happy Clown*, these remaining pieces are arranged by Brown to alternate back and forth, so an Ed story is followed by a Science story which is followed by an Ed story, and so on. The only piece that initially seems an exception is "The Man Who Wouldn't Stop", which seems to be neither. It comes in the place in the pattern where we would expect an Ed story. Thus, because of the pattern already established, we subconsciously suspect it's an Ed story, we know it's relevant, and thus aren't surprised when the first chapter makes the man's inability to stop shitting part of Ed's prison escape.

In other words, Brown is using format to influence how we read "The Man Who Couldn't Stop." That simple pattern of alternation is enough to make us feel it must be relevant to Ed. By carefully picking and choosing from the material from *Yummy Fur* #1-3, Brown imbues the beginning of *Ed* with a kind of intentionality that simply isn't there in *Yummy Fur*. Through deletion, he imposes a sense of order and direction.

The "Introductory Pieces" conclude with "Ed the Happy Clown in Confinement" which, following directly on the heels of "The Man Who Couldn't Stop," breaks the pattern of alternation. But there's also a purpose to such a formatting shift: it suggests we're just doing *Ed* now, that if "Adventures in Science" or any other piece is included in the first half of the issue it will quickly be tied back into the *Ed* story—which is, from here on out in the comics series, the case.

This shaping process was one that occurred well after the original composition process, and it involved suggesting pieces were connected that hadn't originally been thought of as being so. This is true even of the "Adventures in Science" pieces that remain. As Brown suggests in his notes for the 2012 *Ed* about the squid-related "Adventures in Science": "I probably don't need to point out that this 'Adventures in Science' strip wasn't supposed to connect in any way with the 'Ed the Happy Clown' strip that I'd drawn earlier in the year. It was just a goofy comic." (206). And yet now it is connected by implication, even if only introductorily: unlike "Mars" or "City

Swine" it made the cut and became part of *Ed the Happy Clown*.

In his notes to *The Little Man*, Brown makes a distinction between a graphic novel and a serialized ongoing comic. Discussing the one-page comic he wrote in 2006 for the cover of the book—which gives a slightly fictionalized version of his deciding to write "The Toilet Paper Revolt" (from the first *Yummy Fur* mini-comic)—he talks about "a few deliberate inaccuracies" he took in re-envisioning the situation. "I wrote that I was originally planning a 'Toilet Paper Revolt' graphic-novel[9]. What I was actually planning was an open-ended series of comic-books.[10] (Both are long works, the difference is that the creator of a graphic-novel intends to end it.)" (161) It's a curious distinction to make in that it's not that a graphic novel actually *does* end so much as that the creator *intends* to end it. Many of the changes that we see from *Yummy Fur* to *Ed the Happy Clown* seem a retroactive application of intention to the idea of ending. The changes we've spoken of here give a sense from the beginning of the book that the book is going somewhere, has a direction, even a teleology. The changes we'll speak about later—the truncation of the ending in particular—seem to me to reinforce that. They reject the open-endedness and potentially limitless episodic continuance of the Ed story in favor of a discrete Ed story with a definite shape and arc.

In his notes for the 2012 *Ed*, Brown describes this process. "When I began drawing the Vortex issues of *Yummy Fur* I intended to make Ed the focus for my creativity," he begins, suggesting that that focus was not there, or at least not clearly there, in the mini-comic. "What Little Orphan Annie had been for Harold Gray, or Tintin for Hergé, Ed would be for me—a continuing character I'd be drawing for my whole career. I was envisioning that there would be a series of books about Ed, just as there are many Tintin books." (242) Originally, he thought of the end of the Ed installment of *Yummy Fur* #12 ("having

....

[9] Note again his use of the hyphen.

[10] Notice that Brown uses a hyphen here, too, in "comic-books".

Ed drive off newly 'married'") as simply the end of the first album in a series.

The intention at that point was to go on, and potentially to go on endlessly. Indeed Ed did go on for a number of additional issues. But Brown "began to realize that the story had come to its 'natural' end in Y-F[11] #12 and that I was keeping it artificially alive in the subsequent issues." That thinking, coupled with his realization that "A new model was developing for narrative-print-cartoonists—the graphic-novelist model" led to his sense that it might be more productive and satisfying to move a long story to its conclusion and take up a new story. "Maybe I didn't have to only do stories about Ed." (242) This, along with a growing interest in autobiographical stories led him first to quickly come up with an ending for Ed's story in *Yummy Fur* #18, and then later to delete a good part of the later Ed material to offer instead a single focused story. Applying an *intention to end* becomes a kind of revision strategy.

Which raises the question of how much intentionality *Ed* originally had, if any at all. As Brown admits "Most of the Ed story was made up as I went along. I kept coming up with plot ideas and then changing directions when I sat down to draw" (*Ed*, 218). That gives the Ed story a fluidity and a pliability that meshes nicely with its surreal qualities, but also suggests why Brown might have at first gone on beyond what he later thought was its natural end. There's something not so much thoughtless as breathless about the way the Ed story progresses, but also a sense that Brown corrects as he goes, that he's flying by the seat of his pants. Grammel notes how Brown often starts an issue with a flashback but then adds additional material to it. He asks Brown, "Since I've seen this pattern repeatedly I'm curious if this is used to change things you hadn't planned." Brown responds "Yeah, definitely. When I first did issue #4 I didn't know that Ed was in the bushes a couple feet away. So yeah, I'm

----

[11] Notice Brown's very curious use of the hyphen here. Apparently now that *Ed* has become a "graphic-novel", *Yummy Fur* has become *Yummy-Fur*.

adding and changing as I go along. As much as I can." (83)[12]

Of course, even early on in *Yummy Fur*, Brown wasn't doing stories only about Ed: he was also doing his adaptation of *The Book of Mark*. But Brown's gospel pieces had a predetermined shape to them. Moving forward verse by verse, they had a definite structure and a built-in intention to end since the books they are based on do have endings. Which makes it all the more interesting to me that Brown never finished his Gospel sequence, abandoning it before having finished the second gospel.

The weaknesses and strengths of both *Ed* and *Yummy Fur* are derived from the fact that they were written on the cusp of something, that Brown composed them at least partly during a moment when notions about comics were changing. *Yummy Fur* started with its feet squarely in the world of the older notion, that of the continuing character operating over multiple volumes. But by choosing to bring the *Ed* story to a close, Brown was able to forcefully clamber into the newer world of autobiographical comics and the graphic-novel.

Well, kind of. For one thing that's interesting about Brown is what he chooses not to let go of. He continues, despite the large shifts in concern and focus and even mood that occur after he finishes the Ed story, to gather what he does under the rubric *Yummy Fur*. So he starts over, but under the same name, and there are nearly as many post-Ed issues as there are Ed issues (14 as opposed to 18). And when Brown finally does decide it's time to change the name, stops *Yummy Fur* and starts *Underwater*, he picks up the book of Matthew exactly where he left it off—it spans the two comic book series and when Brown shuttered *Underwater* he also stopped working on Matthew.[13] One of the things that makes *Yummy Fur* and *Ed* so

....

[12] Wolk pushes this idea even further, perhaps a little unfairly: "Most of *Ed* after its first few chapters is concerned with picking up the threads of the early sections and trying to make it look like they were always meant to go together." (149)

[13] Brown gives his reasons for stopping *Yummy Fur* in the letters page of its last issue: "In the early summer of 1983 I was about to begin self publishing a comic

Fig. 6. *Yummy Fur #1*, 8:5

interesting is the genuinely complex relationship they have to that particular moment in the development of comics, the way they both do and don't let go of the past and do and don't reach for the future.

As important in the shaping of the "Introductory Pieces" as the alternation between "Adventures in Science" and the "Ed" pieces is what Brown chooses not to include. In *Yummy Fur*, there are pieces that have a similar scatological bent, that focus on sewage, and sewage disposal, in ways that might seem relevant. In particular there's the "The Toilet Paper Revolt" and "Catlick Creek." Not only does Brown choose not to include these pieces in *Ed*, he chooses not to include "Catlick Creek" in *The Little Man* (despite referring to *The*

book of semi-surrealistic strips. I wanted the title to reflect the content and came up with the words YUMMY FUR. Over the years the title of this comic and its contents have drifted further and further apart, and now it's time to admit that the name YUMMY FUR just doesn't suit the book anymore. Now is a good time to change the title because I'm about to begin a new long fictional serial…" That serial, *Underwater*, has remained unfinished.

Little Man as a "virtually complete collection"), nor even mentions in that book that it exists.[14]

"The Toilet Paper Revolt" is a four-page comic told from the perspective of the last man on earth. The title is fairly self-explanatory: toilet paper, presumably tired of being used to wipe asses and then disposed of, has rebelled and killed all humans. The last man is recording a message chronicling humanity's fate when he realizes that he is being hunted by toilet paper. He tries to flee but is attacked by multiple rolls, which wrap themselves around him and asphyxiate him. The last page consists of rolls of toilet paper, talking. (see Fig. 6) At first they are happy ("We sure showed them, huh?" "Yeah! Ha!" "Degrade us will they!" etc.), until one roll asks the question "Now what?" It goes on to ask "What's toilet paper good for anyway? What can we do?!" These questions are met with a panel of silence and a final panel in which only one roll speaks, merely to say "Yeah."

"The Toilet Paper Revolt" has an oblique but still definite connection to the scatological. In addition, it combines the surreal with toilet humor in a way that prepares for the surreal scatology of the Ed story. Including it in "Introductory Pieces" would have given a sense of the Ed story developing from a larger interest in scatology. However, what would have been lost is the clear-cut alternation between "Ed" and "Adventures in Science" that the "Introductory Pieces" currently have.

"Catlick Creek" is a two-page comic that begins *Yummy Fur* #2 (and mini-comic YF#4). It's about a creek near the imaginary town of St. Jukes, Ontario and the farmers whose fields surround it. Since the creek floods annually, a "concerned citizen" of St. Jukes is able to convince the farmers to replace the creek with a drainage ditch,

---

[14] In fact, Brown seems to dislike it enough that he excludes it from the list of what pieces the mini-comics of *Yummy Fur* contained on page 163 of *The Little Man*. He does this somewhat obliquely, by indicating that he's providing a list of "what the first three *Yummy Fur* mini-comics… contained" and just simply not mentioning any from the fourth issue.

Fig. 7 *Yummy Fur #2* 3:8

including a sub-line of the ditch that will drain the septic tanks of the town. Since the farmers, he claims, will benefit, they should be the ones to pay. But once the ditch is dug, the farmers end up with an ugly ditch, devoid of trees, "And without the trees to hold the land the banks are eroding away." To top it all off, the creek still floods, so nothing has changed for the better for the farmers. In St. Jukes, on the other hand, the townsfolk rejoice for being able to drain away their waste matter and for having tricked the farmers into paying for it. (see Fig. 7)

Scott Grammel describes "Catlick Creek" as being one of several of Brown's early stories having "clear cut axes to grind". Brown seems uncomfortable with the piece, which may explain why he has never collected it: "I don't think much of 'Catlick Creek' now… It shouldn't have looked like I was just taking a story from real life and redoing it. It should've worked on its own merits or something." (81) Certainly it has a very different feel than most of the other work in *Yummy Fur*—there's nothing odd or surreal about it, and it seems directly expressive of a political message. At the same time, it's about the politics of waste disposal, something that will become important later in the Ed story when we learn that the reason that the man who couldn't stop couldn't stop is because his anus was being used as a waste disposal system to get rid of an alternate mini-dimension's sewage.[15]

This comes up in chapter five of *Ed the Happy Clown*, when we see

....
[15] It's also worth remembering that a good chunk of *Ed* that takes places in Ed's dimension takes place in the sewers, a more traditional disposal system for sewage.

Fig. 8 *Ed the Happy Clown* 95:3

President Ronald Reagan (who deliberately looks nothing like the actual Ronald Reagan)[16] being consulted by Mister Ding about the national sewage crisis. (see Fig. 8) According to Mr. Ding, "Americans are consuming so much they can't stop shitting!" As a result "the piles of feces are blocking almost every street in Washington and it's the same everywhere in America." Different possible solutions are suggested. Perhaps legislation can be passed limiting Americans to one bowel movement per week, suggests Ding, while Nancy, the president's wife (who also doesn't look all that much like the actual Nancy Reagan), suggests "Wouldn't it make more sense to limit how much a person can consume? And why can't we use the shit for fertilizer anyway?" a comment to which Reagan responds "Nancy, if you don't mind we're trying to have a *serious* discussion."

....

[16] Wolk suggests that "when recognizable people from the real world, drawn realistically, show up in narrative comics, there's always something off-puttingly fake about them." (121) Brown may very well be playing around with this, insisting on the recognizable name Ronald Reagan and then giving us the dissonance of a very different image than the name conjures in our head. Somehow that's less off-putting than an accurate and recognizable Reagan would be. Says Brown, "Since I was going to be drawing an alternate-dimension Reagan who wouldn't even *look* like the real Reagan, I knew that I wouldn't have to worry about actually getting facts right." (*Ed*, 224)

In the middle of this discussion, the gateway to "Dimension X" is discovered and Reagan decides to "solve" the problem by creating a massive funnel and filling it full of fecal matter that will be sent to Dimension X, thus creating the "first inter-dimensional waste disposal site" and curtailing the problem by simply pushing it elsewhere.[17]

By leaving "Catlick Creek" out, Brown ends up making the beginning of *Ed* seem more unified. But, he also removes one of the political resonances of sewage from the work, opting for the surreal over the metaphorical. Both deletions (of "Catlick Creek" and "The Toilet Paper Revolt") opt against providing a broader context in favor of a more unified entry into the story, and both deletions change the way readers are prepared by the introductory pieces to enter the Ed story.

Shit has long been a relevant subject in literature, and it is worth discussing a few of the precursors and analogies to Brown's project. Brown has spoken of that aspect of his work as having been written in response to scatological humor in Japanese manga (something he discusses in his Grammel interview), though he admits in the notes of 2012 *Ed* that it was more of a response to things he'd *heard* about manga rather than anything he'd actually seen. But thinking it was true, Brown became interested in seeing "could I overcome my cultural conditioning and become less squeamish about looking at and creating drawings of feces? I think my reasoning was that using humor to deal with things we're uncomfortable with is better than not dealing with those things at all."[18] (213)

....

[17] This reminds me of the Mobro 4000, a garbage barge that in 1987 was infamous for hauling the same load of trash from Islip, NY along the East coast, trying and failing to dispose of it (it kept meeting quite justifiable resistance from the press, environmentalists and concerned citizens). A version of this barge makes an appearance in Don Delillo's novel *Underworld*.

[18] This is a position similar to those that many who support scatological humor

In the American scene, Robert Crumb violates all sorts of taboos, and many of his early comics are pornographically or scatologically themed. According to Scott Grammel "For years after discovering it, [Brown] was disgusted by the explicit, over-the-top sexuality of Crumb's work. Things change." (66) Brown acknowledges "When I first saw Crumb's stuff I thought it was disgusting, and I didn't like it at all." "[I]t took me still quite a few years to actually be able to look at that stuff and like it." (77) But Brown did learn to respect and admire Crumb and other underground comics artists, and with *Yummy Fur* his own work moved in a similarly transgressive direction.

Freud argues that "The excreta arouse no disgust in children. They seem valuable to them as being a part of their own body which has come away from it."[19] One way of thinking about scatological humor is that it plays the adult's disgust over excreta such as fecal matter, which is culturally constructed, off against the child's delight over it, thus appealing to an earlier stage of our development in a more adult way. There's also Freud's idea of the anal stage as a formative moment for the psychosexual self, and one might think of "The Man Who Couldn't Stop" as the literalization of the "anal explosive" and lack of bowel control. In that case, the response of the mini-dimension to cleaning up their world by tidying away all the shit by forcing it into a tighter and tighter funnel until it literally leaves this dimension is a kind of anal retentive response. What's interesting is that one thing ends up being the inverse of the other, like two sides of the same coin, and the expression of anal retentiveness in one dimension leads to the expression of the anal explosive in the other dimension.

This is not to say that the scatological elements of *Ed* or *Yummy*

---

take. For instance, Ashraf Rushdy suggests "the world would be… a healthier place not when shit is made invisible but when it is confronted as the other we produce." See Ashraf H. A. Rushdy, "A New Emetics of Interpretation: Swift, His Critics and the Alimentary Canal" in *Mosaic* 24.3/4 (1991): 1-32. 29.

[19] Sigmund Freud, *Civilization and Its Discontents*, Trans. James Strachey (New York: Norton, 1961). 52n1.

Fur are an attempt to elucidate Freud any more than that they are a response to actual manga, only that both things figure, in complicated ways, in the construction of the story's scatology. And the connections, I think, are more obvious in *Yummy Fur* than in *Ed* because of the additional pieces: the cover of YF#1, "The Toilet Paper Revolt" and "Catlick Creek".

There's a long history of literary scatology, worth considering so as to think about how Brown does or does not fit in with it. There is James Joyce's *Ulysses* (1922), in which Leopold Bloom spends part of the "Calypso" chapter on the toilet, though, unlike Brown's, Joyce's language is veiled enough that it's hard to see the scene as offensive or, even, truly scatological.[20] The most obvious is François Rabelais, whose *Gargantua and Pantagruel* (1532-1564) is chock-full of scatological humor, including a chapter on Gargantua's invention of a "wipebreech", in his search to discover what works best to wipe's one's ass after shitting. (Spoiler: turns out the very best thing is "the neck of a goose, that is well downed, if you hold her head betwixt your legs."[21]) Rabelais has a kind of playfulness that is similar to Brown's, though has somewhat less of a surreal bent (no doubt because Rabelais died more than three centuries before surrealism).

There's also Jonathan Swift, whose poem "The Lady's Dressing Room" (1732) explores the narrator/suitor's disgust when he realizes that the beautiful Celia has the same sort of plumbing that the rest of us do ("Disgusted Strephon stole away / Repeating in his amorous fits, / Oh! Celia, Celia, Celia shits!"[22]). But this is different too from Brown in that it is fixated (albeit for satirical reasons) on the disgust

....

[20] Though Joyce's letters to his wife Nora do contain some startlingly scatological moments—rapturous reflections on her farts, for instance.

[21] François Rabelais, *Gargantua and Pantagruel*, trans. by Thomas Urquhart and Antony Motteux (Derby: Moray Press, 1894), Chapter 1.XIII.

[22] Swift thought enough of this last line that he had it (and much of the situation) reappear nearly verbatim two years later as the end of another poem, "Cassinus and Peter: A Tragical Elegy."

of having to acknowledge someone's corporeality and any humor is secondary to that—it's not the scatology that causes the humor but the suitor's disgusted reaction that does.

I'll mention just two other writers, these contemporary, and works of theirs written after *Yummy Fur*. They weren't, obviously, an influence after Brown, but do provide a context. In David Foster Wallace's "The Suffering Channel"[23] a shy and damaged Midwestern man shits great and intricate pieces of sculptural poo that are works of art. One of the debates of the story is whether the man has any awareness of what he's doing or if it's somehow being done in spite of him[24]: on one extreme are people who think it must be a trick on the part of the artist or his wife, that the colon couldn't possibly produce such delicate works of sculpture in excrement. On the other is the view that "maybe it's subconscious. Maybe his colon somehow knows things his conscious mind doesn't." (320) Wallace's emphasis is different from Brown's, offering a kind of artistry of poo that partly aestheticizes excrement even while preserving its repulsion (think, for instance, of Andres Serrano's infamous "Piss Christ"). Brown always keeps excrement excremental, but the notion that the subconscious mind is expressed in scatological art is one that I think applies very much to Brown's work.

Gordon Lish's short story "Shit" begins "I like talking about sitting on toilets."[25] This story in particular tells about a time when

....

[23] David Foster Wallace, "The Suffering Channel," in *Oblivion* (New York: Norton, 2004), 238-328.

[24] Wallace's biographer Dan Max describes the character as "a man for whom great art comes so easily he can defecate it," though to me this misses the point of the story, which seems to be partly about how in a way the process has nothing to do with the man himself. See D. T. Max, *Every Love Story Is a Ghost Story: A Life of David Foster Wallace* (New York: Viking Press, 2012), 277.

[25] Gordon Lish, "Shit", in *Collected Fictions* (New York: O/R Books, 2010), 178-180. This is in fact true of Lish's stories and novels: there are an unusual number of moments involving toilets in them.

I couldn't stop going—oh, God, going and going. Forever it felt like.

Gallons it felt like.

It felt like my whole life was coming up and coming up—and going good and out.

…

I thought I was sluicing away, dissolving from the inside out, rendering myself as waste, breaking down to a basal substance, falling through the plumbing, perishing on a toilet I could not even call my own.

You'll laugh, but I got scared. (179-180)

The unnamed narrator ends up getting control of himself by staring at the wallpaper, holding onto the names and representations of the flowers on it as a way of keeping himself from succumbing to panic and of finally being able to stop. But that same feeling of panic strikes me as being analogous to that of the man who couldn't stop.

Finally, in Lish's story "Wouldn't a Title Just Make It Worse?" a narrator named Gordon is staying as a guest at someone's house and just before leaving takes a shit which he finds he can't flush down. He considers various ways to get rid of it and then, panicked that his hosts will discover it, or discover him trying to get rid of it, he eats the turd: "yes, I ate it, you bastards, I ate it! Well, of course, I ate it."[26] (301) The story goes on to speculate on its own fictionality: is it a fiction, is it true, is "Gordon" the same as Gordon? But leaves us in the end, with no answers.

These are all somewhat different pieces than Brown's, but I include

----

[26] Gordon Lish, "Wouldn't a Title Just Make It Worse?" in *Collected Fictions* (New York: O/R Books, 2010), 298-301.

mention of them because I think they all share something with Brown: despite their scatology and humor, there's a sense that there's something serious behind them: a purpose or project as well as a deep-seated anxiety.

That, for me, is what is at the heart of Brown's work as well: the scatology is not purposeless, but directed, even if directed primarily by the subconscious. Brown is thinking with his colon, or letting his colon think for him, but such thinking, when taken seriously, leads not to ribald humor but to a more grotesque sort of laughter. As Jonathan Greenberg notes, glossing Ruskin, the "laughter provoked by the grotesque is always uneasy, nervous laughter, never wholly free from disquiet."[27] For Wolfgang Kayser, the grotesque that starts us laughing also causes that laughter to dry up, making us "feel as if the ground beneath our feet was about to give way."[28] Such is the unsettling condition faced head-on not only by Ed, but by the reader who follows the twists and turns of Ed's story.

....

[27] Jonathan Greenberg, *Modernism, Satire and the Novel* (Cambridge: Cambridge University Press, 2011), 10.

[28] Wolfgang Kayser, *The Grotesque in Art and Literature*, trans. Ulrich Weisstein (New York: Columbia University Press, 1957), 18.

Fig. 9. *Ed the Happy Clown*, 39:1

CHAPTER TWO
SACRILEGE

There is little in the "Introductory Pieces" or even the first chapter of *Ed the Happy Clown* to suggest that the story will soon have prominent Christian religious elements. There is, admittedly, a character named Christian, who appears in "Ed and the Beanstalk" (and who will appear later in the book), but he seems more some sort of zombie than a representative of Christianity. In addition, the second "Adventures in Science" strip offers a parody of the manifestations of Christ's face on various surfaces, with Jesus's face appearing on a piece of masking tape (though in the reproduction of the tape we're given, it's hard to see a face of any kind). Other than that, the words "Jesus" appear only twice and "Jesus Christ" only once in those pages, and are used only as a curse, by Jack in the "Jack and the Beanstalk" story.

With chapter two, however, all this changes. Opening with an image of Mary and baby Jesus, the chapter moves through all sorts of religiously-connected events, surreally mixing together sex and religion, and ending with a murder committed in the name of God.

In the 2012 *Ed*, the chapter opens with a statue of the Virgin and the Baby Jesus, with Jesus holding a severed hand.[1] (see Fig.

....
[1] Brown explains in his notes that this image was used in 1988 as a separate (loose) cover for Vortex's reissue of the first four issues of *Yummy Fur*. (215) By choosing to

9) It's a particularly interesting image in that initially it seems straightforwardly religious; it takes a moment to notice that Jesus is holding a severed hand.

But by the second panel of chapter two, we've moved to the thirteenth century, where we're offered a "Saint's Lives" story about a wife whose husband responds to her interest in having sex with "For some time now I've been thinking we should follow the advise [sic] of the blessed lamb of God and avoid all carnal activities." Instead, he commands her to chop wood outside, which she does, only to see, when she walks past the window, that he is masturbating. The story ends with her cutting off his offending hand.

We then move forward to the twentieth century where we discover that this seems to have been one story from a book called *Lives of the Saints* that is being read by a mother to her three children.

Or maybe not, since the relationship of the 13th century story to the 20th century family is created strictly by juxtaposition. There's a certain amount of ambiguity here. It may be that the book in fact has a changed and sanitized version of the story where Saint Justin "fearing that he would be tempted to resume his criminal activities" has in fact cut off his own hand.[2] But through the ambiguity of juxtaposition, Brown is able to have it both ways: we initially make the leap into thinking that this is a story absurdly being read by a mother to her children, and then step back and wonder if we shouldn't see it as the real story vs. the sanitized version. But the ghost of the first possibility continues to haunt us, as something we can never quite dismiss.[3]

....

use that image for the mega-cover of all four issues, he immediately made readers aware of the importance of *Ed the Happy Clown*'s religious themes.

[2] This apparently isn't the Saint Justin that is best known by that name, the theologian who lived in the second century. Instead, this Saint Justin lived from 1223-1289, and is a saint made up by Brown.

[3] Douglas Wolk reads this scene in a third way, as part of Chet's dream which comes a few pages later, but I don't think there's enough textual evidence to support such a reading—at most it's another ambiguous near-possibility. See Douglas Wolk,

One of the children being read to is Chet, who shares a name with the creator of *Ed*, though Brown has gone out of his way to disavow that a biographical connection exists.[4] Chet has already appeared in "Crime and Punishment with Ed the Happy Clown," where as the night janitor at the hospital he discovers a severed hand only to realize that it's his own hand. Or almost. In a satisfyingly absurd twist, it turns out that though he's missing a hand and has found a hand, it's not *his* hand he's found: he's found someone else's hand that the doctor he consults must have accidentally cut off his patient. Meanwhile, Ed gets punched and loses a tooth, puts the tooth under his pillow and wakes up to find Chet's severed hand in its place. He takes the hand to the police station to turn it in and ends up under arrest. Upon which Chet has the hand, now apparently dead and floppy, sewed back on.

Back to chapter two. After the mother reads saints' lives stories to her children we jump ahead thirty years, to find Chet in monastic robes and praying to a statue of the virgin. In a demonic parody of a miracle, the statue comes alive and they start having sex. When she's coming she calls out "Ooh—Ssaint—Justin!" and tears off Chet's hand, upon which he wakes up: it's been a dream. He tells the dream to Josie, the woman he's cheating on his wife with, and who resembles Mary once she comes alive, who suggests, "Maybe

Reading Comics: How Graphic Novels Work and What They Mean (Boston: Da Capo Press, 2007), 149.

[4] Says Brown in the notes to the 2012 *Ed*: "Chet was not supposed to be me. I gave the character my name because losing my drawing-hand was a paranoid fear I had at the time." So, not him, but yet an embodiment of his fear. Indeed, in the mini-comic Chet originally had "what was supposed to be a southern accent," differentiating him further, though this changed when Brown realized he was going to use the character further, so he "re-lettered his word-balloons to eliminate the accent. It just looked like it was going to be a hassle to keep up." (210-211) Douglas Wolk is dubious: "If this seems pretty fucked up—especially if Chet is meant to be a stand-in for Brown—yes, it is, and it gets more so." (Wolk, 149) And Brown himself admits, about this very scene "Despite my earlier contention that Chet isn't me, this scene is based on memories from my childhood." (217) The relationship of disavowal and identification here is quite complicated.

it contained some kind of clue to why your hand *did* come off the other night." (48)

Later in the chapter Chet pursues Ed, who has been identified as the man who has stolen his hand, into a bookstore. There, his eyes alight on *Lives of the Saints* where he reads again about Saint Justin. He calls Josie to invite her to the park at night. The next time we see them they're having sex, with Josie trying to get Chet to stop babbling and focus on the act and Chet trying to explain that God made his hand fall off to shock him "into recognizing the sinful state... hhh... of my life..." (57) "It's a sin... but you don't want to stop..." answers Josie, whereupon, still *in flagrante delicto*, Chet explains that, like Saint Justin "you have to cut off from yourself the thing that is making you sin." In a shocking series of panels, he cuts Josie's throat, stabs her repeatedly, and then thanks God for allowing him to succeed at cleansing himself from sin.

Though Brown writes in single panels and claims not to think about the page as a unit of meaning, the power of Josie's murder is augmented by the fact that we don't see the knife until we turn the page, and that's the first thing we see. Brown is careful to maintain this page break in both *Yummy Fur* and *Ed*. The first panel is only the blade of a knife, with it not being clear exactly where it's coming from. (see Fig. 10) We share Josie's shock in a way that we wouldn't if the knife was the last panel on page 57 rather than the first panel on page 58 and we could anticipate it. In the next panel we see from over Chet's shoulder as he cuts Josie's throat. The third panel is farther away, at a distance, looking at both of them from behind and to the side of Josie. Then we move closer again, so that we see only Chet's maddened face, the flying blood, and Josie's arm and shoulder. In Panel 5, we're closer still as Chet's hand slips and Josie falls away: we have only Chet's hand, a bit of Josie's arm and a small portion of Chet's face. The final panel is a tight close-up of Chet, still bloody, knife clasped in both hands, praying his thanks to God for a murder successfully carried out and sin defeated. (see Fig. 11)

Fig. 10. *Ed the Happy Clown*, 58:1

Fig. 11. *Ed the Happy Clown*, 58:6

Fig. 12. *Ed the Happy Clown*, 173:8

Later, in chapter three, Brown returns to this scene (page 65 of *Ed*), reliving it this time from a distance and seeing it from a different perspective. At that point we realize that Ed has been beaten up and left in the bushes not far away from where Chet is murdering Josie. The scene continues, with Chet bathing himself clean in an act reminiscent of baptism.

After that, religious context is fairly subdued in *Ed* until, in chapter nine, the now-undead vampire Josie begins looking for Chet at his job in the hospital. She follows him into the hospital grounds and seduces him, but only afterwards does he realize that she's dead. "You've been sent back to tempt me!" Chet cries from beneath her, to which Josie responds "Here's hoping that doesn't count as repentance" and crushes his skull. (173, see Fig. 12) Near the beginning of chapter ten, we find her eating him, and a few moments later Christian joins her, breaking off one of Chet's legs. (177-178)

In the 2012 *Ed* there's one final scene with religious context. After Josie meets her death when Chet's severed hand reappears without explanation and exposes her to sunlight, the final page of the last chapter (chapter twelve) shows Josie and Chet burning in hell, weeping, and pushed by demonic hands into one another's arms. (see Fig. 13) This is a significant change not only from the way the Ed story ends in *Yummy Fur* but from the way it ended the first time it was collected, in 1989. Brown speaks about this in his notes to the

2012 *Ed*:

> [I]n 1992, when it came time to reprint the book, there was a reason I had to tamper a bit with the ending: Josie. The last that we see of Josie in the 1989 version of the book is the scene where she kills Chet at the end of Chapter Nine. That sequence could be seen as an acceptable resolution to her story. Chet seemingly kills her and, in turn, she kills him—traditional revenge-drama stuff. But I couldn't let Josie get away with it. I believe that the impulse for revenge is a negative one, and I felt compelled to make her fate reflect that belief. (243)

It's intriguing to think, considering all the strangenesses of *Ed*—the myriad ways it is potentially offensive, the way it takes apart both political, societal and religious beliefs—that Brown feels so strongly about the morality of letting Josie "get away with it" that he felt he had to kill her off. Yet he does so by letting Chet's hand take revenge. There's an irony here: with Chet Brown both imposing a moral belief on the end of a story that has resisted just that along the way, and doing so by acting through the hand of a man also named Chet. Whether Chet is meant to be Brown in the book as a whole, there's no doubt that Chet's hand and Chester Brown's will are working together

Fig. 13. *Ed the Happy Clown*, 203:3

to bring about Josie's destruction, that in this instance at least the same hand is at work. And not only does Brown kill her off: he could have just as easily stopped Josie's story on page 184, where we know that Chet's hand has exposed her to the sun and can infer what will happen to her next (since we know she's a vampire). Or he could have stopped her story at the first panel of 202, where we see her charred skeleton lying in the bed with Chet's severed hand clinging to the headboard. But instead, Brown chooses to end by bringing them both into hell, asserting both that there *is* a hell and that they are being made to suffer together. Is this togetherness a way of easing their torment or increasing it? It's hard, from these final panels for us to know.[5] [6]

The religious context, you might not be surprised to find out, is different in *Yummy Fur*. Indeed, if we come to the *Ed* story through *Yummy Fur*, instead of feeling that religion appears just early and late in the *Ed* story, we find the *Ed* story surrounded by religion, and as readers of the comic we are constantly being forced to transition from the *Ed* story into a religious story and vice versa.

In addition to the "Adventures in Science" pieces focusing on the piece of masking tape that has the image of Jesus's face on it, there's

....

[5] Though it's ambiguous from context, Brown's personal sense of it is clear: "I should probably let people interpret it as they see fit, but I saw it as part of their punishment."

[6] By contrast, it's interesting to think about what Brown found problematic but didn't change when he moved from *Yummy Fur* to *Ed*. In the notes to *Ed*, he speaks about the rat-eating pygmies that live in the sewer. "Almost immediately after I finished drawing this six page strip [Brown is referring to the first Ed strip, "Ed the Happy Clown"] I considered re-drawing it to eliminate the pygmies, but, since I accepted the surrealist premise, it seemed counter-productive to censor my work to soothe the politically-correct part of my mind" (206). Later, he mentions, when his work was mildly criticized in 1995 for reinforcing old colonial stereotypes, "Reading those words, I felt tremendously guilty." And yet, he chose to leave it as it was. His justification for this is "For what it's worth, I'll add that I now accept Paul Johnson's contention that '"Colonialism" covered such a varied multiplicity of human arrangements that it is doubtful whether it describes any thing specific at all.'" (206)

Fig. 14. *Yummy Fur* #3, 12:4

"I Live in the Bottomless Pit" which Brown chose not to include in the book version of *Ed*. This two-page comic begins with a man hiding out in a cemetery on an island, pursued by people who think "Perhaps we can subdue him by hypnotism." When he's spotted he runs without looking where he's going and ends up falling into the bottomless pit. Again Brown uses the page as a unit to heighten the dramatic effect, having the fall take place on the first page of the comic and the landing in darkness on the second, after the page is turned.[7]

The six panels on the second page all take place in a darkness interrupted only by speech bubbles and the glow of two sets of eyes. The man has survived the fall and finds he's not alone in the apparently not-so-bottomless pit. "Is it time yet?" a voice asks him.

....

[7] This effect is lost when the comic is reproduced in *The Little Man*, since it's printed on facing pages. Admittedly, it's a very small change, but one that lessens the effect of the comic.

"Who are you?" the man asks. "The Anti-Christ," the other voice admits. "Is it time for me to come out yet?" The Anti-Christ goes on to explain: "When God created the world he put me in this pit and told me when I was supposed to come out and everything I was supposed to do." But, he admits, "it's been so long I've forgotten everything he told me." (see Fig. 14)

The idea of the Anti-Christ as someone acting on God's orders is a strange one, one that confounds the opposition between good and evil—in this case the Anti-Christ is following God's plan. There's potentially a kind of gnostic impulse to this idea, though the piece is too short for it to be articulated in any way.[8] In addition, instead of being particularly evil or menacing the Anti-Christ has instead become forgetful and, consequently, ineffectual. He hides in a hole, waiting to do something, but he's forgotten what. He has become absurd.

That absurdity is something that permeates the use of religion in the *Ed* story. Brown has no difficulty both critiquing a Saint story and then suggesting, absurdly enough, that it's the sort of thing to be read to children. He presents Ed's baby sister Annie, who dies falling from the table as her mother reads from *The Lives of the Saints*, first as a kind of benign ghost and then at the end, (see Fig. 15) with little explanation, as a devil.[9] In a dream Chet worships before a statue and then it comes alive and fucks him, which you might read as a commentary on idolatry—though also as a commentary on Chet's troubled state. Josie becomes a vampire, something that doesn't really fit into the Christian mythos—nor does Josie's ability to come back

[8] It's not unlike one of the arguments presented in Jorge-Luis Borges's story "Three Versions of Judas" which suggests that in fact Judas, not Christ, was the personification of God on earth because of the way he moved God's plan forward.

[9] Brown's own claim is that this choice, like much of *Ed*, was initially random: "I wanted to have a ghost explain things to Josie here, and for some reason decided to draw the ghost as a little girl. Initially it wasn't Chet's sister, as can be seen in the original version… After drawing the sequence I decided it might be good if the ghost had a *reason* for hanging around Chet and Josie, so I changed her to Chet's sister." (221)

Fig. 15. *Ed the Happy Clown*, 202:6

from the dead the first time. And the idea of Chet's hand being able
to come back and function to raise the blinds in Josie's room seems
more like something out of a B-horror movie than anything out of
the Christian mythos. And yet, Brown ends with a vision of Josie
and Chet burning in hell that seems sober and straightforward.[10]
Nothing about religion in *Ed* or *Yummy Fur*, then, should be taken
for granted, and Brown is exceptionally deft at muddying the waters
in a way that makes it very hard to pin him down as either believer
or satirist, as either anti-religionist or apologist—as, in short, any
one thing. These contradictions and tensions, and the way they feed
back into subconscious fears and desires, are one of the things that
make *Ed the Happy Clown* so interesting.

But there's a level of contradiction and complexity that's left out
of *Ed the Happy Clown*, and it's that material in particular that I,

----

[10] It's worth noting that Chet's hand is still missing when he's in hell. It's as if
the hand, despite exposing Josie to sunlight and destroying her, continues to 'live'.
Brown let the hand get away with it, even if he didn't let Josie get away with it.

and so many other readers, found the most shocking the first time we read *Yummy Fur*. YF#4 was the first issue to consist of material not found in the mini-comics, and was Brown's chance to determine the direction of the serial comic as a whole. He might have simply done the *Ed* story and focused in exclusively on that. Or he might have continued to do a number of short pieces to go with the now-developing *Ed* story, as he'd done in the mini-comic. Instead, though, he decided to split the issue into two continuing stories, something he will do in almost all the remaining issues of *Yummy Fur*.[11]

There's nothing inherently unusual about this; indeed, it was a practice followed by a lot of people writing floppies as a way of not putting too much pressure on a single story. What's unusual, though, is Brown's choice for his secondary story. After 19 pages of *Ed* that document Chet's childhood obsession with saints and the effect it has had on him in later life, culminating in his brutal murder of Josie *in the name of religion*, Brown offers 6 pages entitled "Mark, Part One: The Beginning of the Good News of Jesus Christ." (see Fig. 16)

What follows is a quite faithful and methodical retelling of the Gospel of Mark, Chapter 1, verses 1-39. You might expect, considering the story we've just read, for it to be a retelling that questions or undermines the gospel, but Brown approaches the gospel at a certain remove, with a great deal of constraint and control. At this stage, the drawing style is different from *Ed* or from the short pieces in YF#1-3, with certain of the panels resembling tableaux from a traditional book of Bible stories, and with most of the panels depicting events from a distance, rather than the close-ups we often have in Ed—a distance Brown will increasingly opt for in his later work, such as *Louis Riel*. There's nothing ironic about it in *Mark*, though at the same time, it doesn't seem particularly spiritual. In fact, it's a little hard to know what to make of it exactly, particularly at this stage.

....
[11] The exceptions are #18 (which is exclusively the Ed story, which it finishes), #23 (exclusively *Disgust*, which it finishes), #28 (exclusively *Fuck*), and #30 (exclusively *Fuck*, which is finishes).

Fig. 16. *Yummy Fur* #4, 20:1

Brown says of the choice not to tell the story in a way that might offend Christians, "I felt that that kind of would have been expected of me. People were expecting me to do something weird with Mark." (Grammel, 86) Since a traditional retelling is precisely what we don't expect, it comes across as weirder than something truly weird would be, because it makes us shift our expectations as readers, taking away what we thought we knew about Brown as a storyteller.

This faithful but flat retelling is somehow a great deal more shocking than a more transgressive interpretation might be. The contrast between *Mark* and *Ed* couldn't be more pronounced, and as readers we're forced to quickly switch gears in a way that can't help but strip them, being confronted by a soberly Christian text on the heels of a murder committed for religious reasons. It does seem a strange choice, either as if Brown wants the reader to run the full gamut of views on religion or as if, feeling that he's pushed *Yummy Fur* uncomfortably far, he wants to balance it against something quite different. But it's much more troubling to have the Mark story there since the contrast is so great; the transition feels, especially for someone who grew up staunchly Christian, almost as if your

Sunday School teacher had just walked in on you while you were masturbating.

I have to think that Brown understands the strength of this juxtaposition, and that he both enjoys and is disturbed by this effect. In Issue #6, he places his letters page (called *The Fur Bag*) not at the end of the issue but in between *Ed* and *Mark*, insulating one from the other.[12] This is the first time Brown has a letters page, and thus the first time since he started doing exclusively *Ed* and *Mark* that he has other material.[13] That his first impulse is to stick it between the two stories is quite significant. It gives the reader a breather in a way that we haven't had with the transition before. However, he does this only this once, which makes it so we have this one moment where the reading experience changes and we can catch our breath. Which, paradoxically, makes us more conscious of the fact that we haven't had that breather before, and won't get it later.[14]

Fig. 17. *Yummy Fur #29*, 22:1

As the *Gospel of Mark* continues and then finishes, to be replaced by the *Gospel of Matthew*, things about it begin to change, as if the

[12] When I asked Brown about this, he responded "[A]ny answer I give would be a guess. Perhaps I wanted to feature the letters page prominently in the sixth issue since none of the previous issues had one." It is worth noting, too, that it wasn't an uncommon practice in comics in the 1970s to put the letters page in the middle (some issues of *Conan*, for instance, did this). Perhaps it was an homage to that.

[13] Well, kind of. At the end of YF#5 there's a brief comic announcing that Brown is opening a letters page and describing what comics he likes. This he does at the end of the issue rather than in between the two continuing stories.

[14] In later issues the *Fur Bag* is most often at the end, though in several issues (YF#7 for instance), it appears at the beginning of the issue.

ideas of one half of *Yummy Fur* are starting to bleed into the other—though just barely. By the time we get to Part 2 of *Mark in* YF#5, Jesus has started looking less like the traditional serene representation of himself common in Western Christianity. His hair is often deranged, and in some panels he looks disgruntled. Later, he often looks quite angry and shouts even more. (see Fig. 17) Jesus and his disciples look more and more Semitic. By the time Brown is well into *Matthew*, in YF#25 (having finished *Mark* in YF#14), things start to change even more dramatically. He's started to break the frame a little, to upset the story. Matthew, for instance, is depicted as someone who picks his nose. We get a far from flattering sense of several of the disciples. The pacing changes, with Issue #26 offering just one verse per page, leaving room for more visual interpretation. By YF#27, it's slowed down even further, with three pages used to depict a single verse.

The bleed doesn't really go the other way in *Yummy Fur*: the Ed story doesn't seem to be taking on the sobriety of the bible stories as it progresses; it remains consistently strange, surprising and weird.

However, there is one possible exception to that. When Brown puts together the definitive Ed book, he cuts a good portion of the last several issues of the *Ed* story, which does make it more unified if not exactly more sober. And, as I've already mentioned, he draws a final few pages, in which Josie and Chet burn in hell together, that didn't exist in the earlier version. As with the early pages of *Mark*, this seems a sincere and non-ironical depiction, something meant to be taken at face value, which is a very odd way to end a graphic novel which has been full of surreal twists and turns. In my opinion, this gesture on Brown's part has a function not unlike what he achieved by juxtaposing the gospels to *Ed*: it shifts the way we read, and does so in a way that we don't expect. In this case, it shifts it profoundly enough to close the book. Could it be that Brown, having lost the interaction with the gospels when he moved the Ed story from *Yummy Fur* to *Ed the Happy Clown*, was subconsciously trying to capture the unsettling feeling that having *Ed* and the gospels juxtaposed had offered his readers?

Fig. 18. *Yummy Fur #13*, 6:5

CHAPTER THREE
LOST PAGES
The Discarded Ed Material

By far the most significant shift from *Yummy Fur* to *Ed* involves the Ed material that Brown chose to cut in making *Ed the Happy Clown* into a "graphic-novel". This is largely a matter of truncation: a few panels are dropped or cropped or redrawn earlier in the *Ed* story, but the vast majority of changes consist of Brown's decision to conclude Ed's personal story at the moment when Becky Backman takes Ed, rather than her husband Bick, home from the hospital. Through this decision, Brown ends up making most of the Ed material in *Yummy Fur* #13-18 irrelevant. In other words, *Ed the Happy Clown* cuts around a third of the Ed material that is to be found in *Yummy Fur*. In addition, as discussed above, for the revised book version of *Ed the Happy Clown* Brown writes a new ending to Josie and Chet's story, putting them both in hell together.

There's also some rearrangement of the material that is saved: the eleven pages of the Ed story that Brown saves from YF#17 are moved between material found in YF#11 and YF#12. The material in YF#12 concluded the first book-length Ed volume, though all later versions have an additional four pages.

The differences between *Yummy Fur* and *Ed* are something like this[1]:

WHAT PARTS OF *YUMMY FUR* MAKE IT INTO *ED THE HAPPY CLOWN*

YF #1: No material included in *Ed*. (22 pages left out)

YF #2: Approximately 13 pages of material included in *Ed*. (11 pages left out)

YF #3: 19 pages of material included in *Ed*. (5 pages left out)

YF #4: All of Ed material included (19 pages). All of *Mark* left out. (6 pages)

YF #5: Except for first panel on inside cover, all of Ed material included (18 pages). All of *Mark* material left out. (7 pages)

YF #6: Except for one transitional panel at the end of the Ed material, all of Ed material included (17 pages). All of *Mark* left out. (6 pages)

YF #7: All of Ed material included (17 pages). All of *Mark* left out. (7 pages)

YF #8: All of Ed material included (12 pages). All of *Mark* left out. (10 pages)

YF #9: All of Ed material included (17 pages). All of *Mark* left out. (6 pages)

YF #10: All of Ed material included (18 pages). All of *Mark* left out. (5 pages)

....

[1] I'm not cross-referencing here the mini-comic since it's reproduced in full in YF #1-#3 and since I've discussed that to some degree above. I'm also not here focusing on the covers for the issues vs. the Chapter "covers" for the graphic novel, though I will discuss that later. I've also chosen not to talk here about the Fur Bag (the letters section), though of course that has an effect on the feel and shape of the reading experience as well. I also am not documenting small panel changes, though I will discuss some of these below.

YF #11: All of Ed material included (14 pages). All of *Mark* left out. (9 pages)

YF #12: All of Ed material included (15 pages). No *Mark* included. (10 pages)

YF #13: None of this Ed material included (13 pages). All of *Mark* left out. (11 pages)

YF #14: None of this Ed material included (9 pages). All of *Mark* left out. (13 pages)

YF #15: None of this Ed material included (12 pages). All of *Matthew*[2] material left out. (11 pages)

YF #16: None of this Ed material included (18 pages). All of *Matthew* left out. (~5 pages)

YF #17: Some Ed material included (11 pages), some left out (4 pages). All of *Matthew* left out. (9 pages)

YF #18: None of the Ed material included. (24 pages)

In other words, to make his 203-page 2012 edition of *Ed the Happy Clown*, Brown excludes a total of 38 pages of introductory material and 80 pages of material directly related to Ed. A third of the material that Brown wrote and originally published in *Yummy Fur* in relation to Ed is left out. Even if we choose to discount the introductory material in the first few issues (it came early, Brown was still figuring out what he was doing, etc.) and not count it, Brown leaves out well over a quarter of the original Ed story.

....

[2] At this point, having finished the gospel of Mark, Brown begins the gospel of Matthew. There's something interesting about Brown's page numbering. For the Ed material, the first four issues were unnumbered. After that, he begins to number each Ed supplement anew with each issue. The Mark material, however, is continuously numbered, with the numbering continuing from the issue before it. Starting with Matthew, however, Brown starts simply numbering the whole issue from beginning to end, restarting the numbering with each new issue. Is there a significance to this? Hard to say.

In addition, in moving from *Yummy Fur* to *Ed the Happy Clown*, Brown leaves out all the gospel stories, amounting to 90 pages of *Mark* and the first 25 pages of *Matthew*. Taking everything into account, Brown takes the first 18 issues of *Yummy Fur*, boils it down from around 436 pages to 203 pages, and ends up with *Ed the Happy Clown*.

Perhaps this last statement is a little unfair, in the sense that both *Mark* and *Matthew* are clearly separate stories, graphic novels in their own terms—or at least *Mark* is: *Matthew* was never quite finished so can only be seen as something on the way to a graphic novel that was abandoned en route. After declaring for some time that he would eventually finish it, Brown stated in 2011 "it wouldn't be that difficult to finish Matthew at this point, because I'm not that far from the end. I'm at the point where Jesus is just about to enter Jerusalem, which is his last days, and it's leading right up to the crucifixion. But my heart just isn't in it. I have no interest now in finishing it. There's other stuff I'd rather do."[3]

But in any case, there would be no real justification to include them in *Ed the Happy Clown*. At the same time, the only form in which we have Brown's *Mark*—which *is* finished—is *Yummy Fur*, where it exists in relation to the Ed story. Even though it is finished, Brown has chosen never to publish it in book form.[4] Since I've argued above about what it is that the juxtaposition with the gospels does for the

[3] Quoted in Sean Rogers, "A John's Gospel: The Chester Brown Interview" *The Comics Journal* (May 9, 2011), http://www.tcj.com/a-johns-gospel-the-chester-brown-interview/

[4] This despite announcing in *Yummy Fur* #25 "Keep your eye out for a book collection of my *Mark* adaptation to be published by Vortex later this year." Brown's explanation for this to me was: "Bill never paid me for the second edition of the Ed book, so I wasn't anxious to let him publish something else. There are no plans to reprint Mark or finish Matthew." At the same time, it does seem Brown would be in a position to publish *Mark* if he so desired. One curious thing about Brown is the degree to which he's chosen not to finish and/or publish in book form a significant chunk of his output that has appeared in comics. The unfinished *Underwater*, for instance, and *Mark*, and *Matthew*.

Ed story and how the reading experience changes without them, I won't repeat that here.

Putting the question of the gospels aside, Brown still leaves a great deal of his originally published Ed material out of the book version. Why?

Originally Brown thought Ed might go on for even longer. In "The Fur Bag" in YF#19 he explains: "I only realized I was wrapping up the Ed saga while I was halfway through writing and drawing YF#17. (I think I was on page nine.) This would have been late June and the Ed book was too far into production to pull. Still we can always print a second Ed book reprinting 13-18 sometime or other. The orders for the book at hand, though, have been so ridiculously low that we're not anxious to rush into print with another one." So, the ending initially surprised Brown. But later, he began to feel that he'd not ended the story soon enough: "The story came to a natural end with the twelfth issue. I was keeping the story artificially alive past that point." This may well be true, but seems strangely appropriate for a story in which one of the main characters, Josie, keeps coming back from the dead: there's something about the extended version of Ed that echoes the absurdity of certain situations in the book itself. Nevertheless, at this point Brown has for a number of years been quite insistent that the book version of Ed, which has been essentially the same since 1992's "the definitive Ed book", is the right one, the version he wants to survive.[5] Indeed, when I asked him how he would feel knowing the *Yummy Fur* version of *Ed the Happy Clown* would be lost to readers, he responded with just one word: "Happy."[6]

....

[5] Which makes Douglas Wolk's 2007 assertion that "It's not surprising that Brown can't seem to settle on a conclusion, because there can't actually be a definitive form of *Ed*" (150) a strange one. Wolk is too invested in his own belief in *Ed*'s unfinishability—"It's unfinishable, because finishing it would mean some kind of narrative closure…"—to acknowledge that Brown has been consistent for more than 20 years about what is the definitive version of *Ed*.

[6] I should say that rightly or wrongly I want to read Brown's response as having

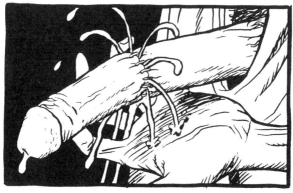

Fig. 19. *Yummy Fur #13*, 9:5

   In the later *Yummy Fur* Ed material that the book will drop, Brown
moves past the traumatic events that have characterized the poor
misunderstood Ed since we first met him. At the end of issue twelve
we see him still unconscious and on the seat of the car as Mrs.
Backman drives him home. She has been told that Ed is her husband.
She's suspicious of this—he doesn't look like her husband—but the
doctors explain he's had a nose job and some other work done as
well.

   In the 13 Ed pages of #13 (subtitled "Saturday Morning (and
Friday Evening)" on the cover), we first move back slightly in time.
We see Bick Backman say goodnight to his two daughters, then his
wife comes to tell the girls that they'll be out that night (for Bick's
penis enlargement). The next morning Ed wakes up looking anxious,
in bed with Becky Backman. She explains to her daughters "I took
daddy into the hospital last night and he had a few operations so he
looks different now", but her explanations are cut short when Ed is
attacked by the family dog Woofer, who resembles somewhat the
larger dog in Brown's "Fire with Fire" comic from YF#2. Neither the

a certain amount of irony to it, particularly considering that it references his title
character and that Ed the Happy Clown seems anything but happy. At the same
time, Brown has been very consistent since the publication of "The Definitive Ed
Book" in 1992, more than 20 years ago, in wanting to discard the later Ed material.

dog nor the girls are buying the idea that Ed is Bick ("Our Father?" asks the oldest, "Where's our *real* father?"), though Becky forces them to hug "their father." Ed doesn't speak at all for the first 7½ pages, listening anxiously like a trauma victim to what Becky says and not responding to either her or the children. When he does finally speak (panel 8:6) it's to ask if he can go to the bathroom and then to ask where it is. "You know where it is!" says Becky. "Right over there."

What follows is one of the most disturbing scenes in the Ed story, in which Ed tries to pee and finds that his penis leaks where it's been grafted together. (see Fig. 19) He manages to wrap it in toilet paper and gets it to work sufficiently. Between that and an earlier scene in which an erection puts intense pressure on his stitches (4:3-5), there's a lot of penis trauma here, as well as a sense that Ed's cock just isn't quite working.

Meanwhile the girls decide to slip out and call the police to "ask them to make mom bring daddy back". Becky and Ed go separately in pursuit of them. Later Becky finds Ed juggling and doing other clown tricks to entertain the girls. He has gained their approval: "Mom, let's keep this Daddy! He's way better than the other one—he can do *all kinds* of tricks!" Becky, though, remains in denial about Ed not being Bick, still trying to justify and explain away his odd behavior.

YF#14 goes further back in time, introducing us to Blanche and Tom, Becky's parents, shortly after Blanche has given birth and while she's waiting to see her baby. Then we jump forward to Blanche visiting Becky's family, with the children excited to introduce her to their new daddy. When she sees Ed, she's incredibly shocked and has to retreat with Becky to lie down, much to the children's confusion. Ed's asked to make tea, to which he responds, "How do you make tea?" Back in the past, the doctors bring Blanche her baby girl, only to have her discover that she's been given a baby boy. The doctors claim that they've made a mistake but Blanche is insistent—this is

Fig. 20. *Yummy Fur #14*, 9:1

Fig. 21. *Yummy Fur #15*, 3:1

her baby! It looks like her! But they take the baby away from her, despite her protests.

Becky, listening to the story in the present, asks "You mean… I'm not really your daughter?" But Blanche sees it differently: she knows that Becky is her daughter as well, and is sure that she had twins but that the doctor sold the boy. Thus, Ed is Becky's twin. After this, Becky is sure that Ed's not Bick, but since the penis-enlargement operation was illegal she knows the hospital won't acknowledge their mistake. Since the family is dependent on Bick's job, she and her mother decide the only thing that the can do is disguise Ed as Bick (see Fig. 20) and carry on as if nothing has changed, which they manage only somewhat successfully.

In issue #15, we return to the aliens that we've seen very early in the Ed story, way back in "Ed and the Beanstalk". The aliens are intrigued by the fact that humans seem to live by a seven-day cycle, entering certain buildings (churches, though the aliens don't know that) on the seventh day. One of the aliens plans to disguise himself in human clothes and investigate. Back with Ed, (see Fig. 21) Becky has made a new, better nose for him and is drilling him and the girls on how to respond to questions at church ("Remember girls—don't tell anyone that this isn't really daddy."). Despite the faultiness of Ed's disguise, the only one to question it is Janet, the children's babysitter, who asks "Hi Mister Backman. Gee, what happened to your nose?" But Ed's explanation, "Uh—Uhm—S-Surgery," immediately satisfies her. Everybody else, though, accepts Ed as Bick, since he occupies Bick's role. We get the distinct sense that maybe nobody pays attention to who people actually are, only to what space or role they occupy. Of all the scenes in the entire Ed story, this one deals most strongly with the relationship of the community to the individual and suggests something profoundly troubling, and yet quite incisive and relevant, about the relationships of our selves and our bodies to the social roles that we occupy and that in a sense stand in for us.

Having listened to the sermon, the alien remains thoughtfully seated after the church service is finished. Since Ed and Becky and Blanche are counting takings in the collection plate, the daughters are left alone with him. When Kari, the youngest girl, interacts with him (see Fig. 22), he asks "Is it true you humans have found a way of living forever?" He goes on to mention that the sermon has said that if you have the love of Jesus inside you, you will live forever. Priscilla, the older daughter, answers, "Oh yes, that's true." Misunderstanding what this actually means, the alien abducts the two girls and takes them to his flying saucer to try to learn the secrets of immortal life.

In #16, we jump to the White House, but not the White House in the micro-dimension: this time it's the White House in our world. Reagan and Nancy are watching religious TV and she begins to erotically suck the puss out of a blister on his heel. On the flying saucer, the Backman daughters are explaining their religion, how Jesus "died and went up to heaven and then he came back down." The aliens decide to throw them out of the saucer to see if they really can't die ("There is only one way to test what she is saying."). When they have Kari cornered, Priscilla begins to pray to Jesus to protect them,

Fig. 22. *Yummy Fur #15*, 10:5

Fig. 23. *Yummy Fur #16*, 16:4

but who shows up is not Jesus but Frankenstein, who apparently has taken up skydiving. (see Fig. 23) Jump to Reagan fucking Nancy from behind, their sex interrupted by word that they've just brought "some guy down from Canada who's supposed to have a penis that looks like me." Nancy's response is "Hahahahahha—show me a man who doesn't have a penis that looks like you!" but she's still interested in seeing it. Bick Backman is in a box, very feverish, saying the phrase "It talks" over and over again. The penis is pus-swollen, and Nancy seems intrigued by this. Mister Ding, the man who brought the box in, accidentally lets his crowbar slip and knocks Reagan out. With Reagan unconscious and Ding going for help, Nancy is free to drag Bick into the other room, tie him down and begin sucking the pus out of the penis, only to find when she does so that the penis begins to talk and calls her by name. Just then, she is called away to talk to a doctor. Cut back to Frankenstein, who parachutes to earth with the Backman girls holding to his feet. He just happens to land at the White House, and the girls wander in to find their naked, bound daddy.

In issue #17 (some of which is reproduced in *Ed the Happy Clown*), we begin with a pygmy running madly through the sewer. He's caught by Christian and strangled to death. Christian is about to eat him when he notices Josie nearby him in the bushes, her face bloody, apparently feeding off the dead Chet. "Oh boy—real food!" Christian says. "Do you mind if I join you?" He breaks off one of Chet's legs and digs into it, while Josie continues to bite Chet's neck. Soon, she excuses herself and goes in search of Ed. When she doesn't find him (impossible she would, since Ed is now elsewhere), she turns into a bat and flies home. Meanwhile, Christian continues eating, but notices when one of Chet's hands detaches itself from the dead man's arm and scuttles off.

At home, Josie's mother is busy having sex with a muscle-bound younger man, who, after Josie arrives, she tries to set up with her. There's a nicely absurd tension between the kind of typical conversation a mother and a daughter might have about the guy the former is trying to set the later up with ("What's the matter with him?" "Nothing mum, he's just not my type.") and the fact that all three are naked, and that the mom has just been having sex with the man. Josie goes to bed, taping up her blind and falling asleep. In panel 10:5, Chet's severed hand appears without explanation, loosens the taped down blind, and raises it while Josie sleeps on.

Jump to the next morning. Josie's mother and the muscle-bound guy are having coffee together now and talking. "She didn't seem too interested in me last night," he suggests. "It was just that she was so tired," the mother responds, and encourages him to go into her bedroom and "wake her up with a kiss." When he does, he finds her on fire, in the process of being burned by the sun. They drag her into the bathtub and soak her down, then carry her through the apartment building, planning to drive her to the hospital. But as soon as they get into the sun she catches fire. She scrambles screaming to a manhole cover and dives into the sewer. The mother

Fig. 24. *Yummy Fur #17*, 15:2

sends the potential boyfriend down in after her (see Fig. 24), upon which the Ed portion of the issue ends.

Neither the boyfriend nor the mother will reappear, and it's puzzling as to why Brown might include this last moment of suggested searching at all: it's a little bit as if he had a plan for something to happen with the boyfriend in the sewers but then abandoned it. The majority of YF#17, pages 1-11, are included in *Ed*, but are also moved forward. They become chapter ten, between the Ed material from YF#11 (chapter nine) and the Ed material from YF#12 (chapter eleven). None of the material in YF#17 is included in the 1989 version of the Ed book, no doubt because it was already in production when Brown was working on YF#17, so that earlier version simply follows the order of the comics (with the changes already mentioned in the introductory pieces), moving from YF#1 to YF#12, ending with Ed asleep in Becky's car. The biggest change in the definitive version of Ed—apart perhaps from the new Hell-related material added at the very end—is this splicing in of eleven

Fig. 25. *Yummy Fur #18*, 2:6

pages of material from YF#17 within the already existing framework of the 1989 graphic novel, and the abandoning of all other Ed-related material in YF#13 to YF#18.

In YF#18, Brown wraps the Ed story up, covering quickly most of the major figures still remaining after Josie and Chet's story has concluded. It starts with Christian returning home with a bag of dead pygmies. As he dumps them into his deep freezer, he hears a beeping sound coming from a valise. He opens it and inside we see a spy-style video transmitter, on which someone who looks like a hollow-eyed Mr. Clean appears (see Fig. 25), saying "Agent Christian, we are recalling you." The next panel (3:1) indicates that he is transmitting from space. This is the first moment that we have a sense that Christian might be working for someone other than himself, let alone that he is an extraterrestrial agent. It gives a context to Christian's existence and his motivations that isn't to be found in the book version of *Ed*.

The next night, Christian goes down into the gutter to hunt pygmies, where he finds Josie. Her hair has been burnt off and she's naked, but still alive, apparently recovered from being burnt by the sun. Christian offers her his apartment, since he's leaving the planet, and together they hunt pygmies. On the way back he points out a flying saucer; Josie asks "Is it one of yours?" to which he responds "No, that's not a Martian ship. That's one from a planet called Earth." When Josie questions this he answers "A *different* planet Earth." In just a few panels, then, Christian is identified as being from Mars and we are also presented with the idea of another alternate earth in addition to the mini-earth that we've already seen.[7]

Back at home, they pack the pygmies into the freezer and then Josie tapes up the windows. They settle down to watch TV, Christian snacking on a pygmy as he watches. By the next morning, Josie's hair has started to grow back. Christian introduces her to his landlady, suggesting that she take over the apartment, and then they return to the apartment just in time to see Ed on TV, posing as Bick Backman in front of the church that was destroyed by aliens. Josie and Christian are each surprised to discover that the other knows Ed, and Christian in addition states something that gives us a little bit of insight into Ed: "He's not wearing his clown make-up. He becomes disoriented when he's not wearing it." In a coincidence that stretches believability to the breaking point, Josie happens to remember that her cousin Janet babysits the Backmans' kids. Josie telephones her and gets a sense of what's going on. Janet also reports that she just had a weird call from Backman's daughters, claiming that they were brought by a saucer to Washington D.C. and that they're claiming to be with Nancy Reagan.

At midnight that night, Christian and Josie are picked up by

....

[7] This is largely inference on my part, but since the spaceship isn't tiny or commented on as being small, it doesn't seem to be from the mini-dimension that we already know. Thus, a third earth…

a flying saucer. But instead of going to Mars they head instead to Washington DC, where they find Nancy Reagan lying in bed with a still-bound Bick Backman. The children meantime are being kept in the White House dungeon. Josie and Christian brave a confrontation with the military (see Fig. 26) to rescue the children and then fly them back home, restoring them to their beds and replacing Ed

Fig. 26. *Yummy Fur #18*, 16:5

with Bick before flying away. Christian puts Ed's clown make-up back on and Ed thanks him. Then they drop off Josie. "Good night, Ed. I'll see you soon," she says. Last stop before Mars is to drop off Ed at his apartment. (see Fig. 27)

Ed sleeps, feels much better, even finds that his penis doesn't hurt quite as much as it did the day before. He decides to go to the "clown agency" to see if they have a job for him, but on the way there he sees Josie's house on fire and discovers that she has been burnt to a crisp—she is nothing but a pile of charred bones now which, strangely enough, is holding Chet's unburned and undamaged severed hand. The penultimate panel of the issue shows Ed striding away dressed again as a clown, mirroring our first introduction to him many issues before. The final panel, taking up the bottom 2/3rds of the page, is nothing but flames, perhaps meant to represent the burning house, or perhaps meant to represent the fires of hell.[8]

If we see it as the latter, then perhaps this provides the explanation for why Brown might have included the final scene in hell in the

....

[8] Brown confirms: "Yes, that's supposed to be the fires of hell at the end of YF 18." But the way it's presented it seems like a reader could see it as either.

Fig. 27. *Yummy Fur #18*, 21:4

definitive version of the graphic novel. Hell was inferred or implied at the end of YF#18, but subtly enough for it not to stick with the reader. By making the emphasis on religion and hell more insistent in the final version, perhaps Brown was merely making explicit something that was already implicitly there.

It is true that the graphic novel version of *Ed* is tighter and more focused and, perhaps, holds together as a book more. With Brown thinking initially of *Ed* as something he would potentially work on for his whole career, the second discarded part of the Ed story makes more sense: it could be a second Ed book, which would then be followed by a third, then a fourth and so on, with Ed moving haplessly from one absurd situation to another. It has much of the surreal weirdness of the first part, though there's been a shift toward questions of identity and domesticity as well, so it has a mood that feels very much connected to the earlier Ed material but that begins to move in other directions, as if each potential Ed album might well have had a different focus.

But when Brown realized that he'd in fact reached the end of the Ed story with YF#18, everything changed. Now instead of having the first two books in a continuing series of albums, he had one longer book and another shorter one, two parts that both did and didn't balance well in relation to one another. I can imagine that is why it both felt satisfying initially to reach an end but quickly came to seem just not quite right. One book that was 198 pages (as the 1989 version of the Ed book is), then another that was 80? On a formal level it doesn't feel quite right, and even if they were brought together, there's no changing the fact that Ed's story goes through a radical shift with YF#13 once he goes home with Becky Backman. But certainly with much of the story already published, it must have seemed increasingly to Brown like the later Ed material was an afterthought, and that, already having turned toward more autobiographical material, he was ready to simply let the later Ed material go rather than reinforcing people's sense of him as a surreal cartoonist telling transgressive fictional tales.

Ultimately, though, I'd argue that what's happened here is another shift in format, and that his new understanding of what he's writing—or rather his retroactive understanding of what he *was* writing—ends up making the decision for him. Brown begins by thinking he is writing a mini-comic—something that he'll compose in his spare time while working a so-called real job and then hock by hand: either on the streets or by going from store to store and convincing them to carry it on consignment. It makes sense that the pieces for such an endeavor would be short and not necessarily serial: he can't count on people reading the issues in order or even on their being able to find the early issues once he's moved on to the later ones.

That goes well enough that someone invites him to try it as a comic, with more pages per issue, warehousing, and a distribution system. His initial response to this is simply (perhaps largely—or even entirely—because of the arrangement he struck with the publisher, but also because it keeps him from having to draw new material) to republish the mini-comic just as is, cramming several mini-comics into each of the first three issues. That must have been quite satisfying, but it also causes some confusion as well, with *Yummy Fur #1* containing the mini-comics *Yummy Fur #1, #2* and *#3*. It's as if Brown is using the comic to memorialize the mini-comic. Certainly he could have kept the same material but approached it differently, in a way that took advantage of the new form. But he doesn't.

Until he gets to the fourth issue. Here, there's a shift, a sense that yes, he's pinched himself, and this is not a dream: he's got a contract to do a serial comic book! Now suddenly he *does* begin to take advantage of the form, employing it formally in a way that readers have seen in other comic books: primary story, secondary story.[9] Eventually he even puts together a letters page. There are moments, though, when we find Brown consciously or subconsciously rebelling against this form—little cracks: putting the letter page in the middle of an issue, for instance, or using the letters page as a political platform (as in Issue #9), or beginning to use the letters page to provide notes as well, or even messing around a bit with the page numbering. But, basically, he's writing an ongoing comic and is aware of it.

Now here is where it gets tricky. Brown is writing an ongoing comic at a moment where there's beginning to be a sense that ongoing independent comics can become graphic novels and be published in book form, and that this might even make the comic subsidiary to the book. At the same time, Brown is aware of another, earlier tradition, the tradition of the comics album, such as we see with Hergé's *Tintin*, for instance: multiple adventures with the same characters in them, each volume of which has its own shape and direction and which may have a loose directionality (i.e. you should read this one before that one) but in which rarely do events from one

---

[9] Brown spoke to me about the reason for this change, disavowing that it was brought on by format considerations: "I knew I'd have to produce quickly to put out six issues a year, so I decided that continuing stories made sense, rather than beginning something new each issue. It wasn't the floppy format that pushed me to do continuing stories, it was the need to produce relatively quickly."

volume become something you have to know to understand major (and even minor) events in a later volume (or if you do, Hergé is kind enough to label them as "Book 1" and "Book 2" or simply to give a brief reference at the bottom of the page). An album and a graphic novel seem, at least superficially speaking, alike—they're both long and they both, within their pages, have a clear arc, plot, and development. However, graphic novels have a tighter directionality, each part is dependent on the others and they are written with a sense of progression and coherence. You can't really take two stories that might serve as separate albums in an ongoing series and make them into a graphic novel, because it simply won't have the right shape—it will feel too episodic, too picaresque.[10]

....

[10] It's worth mentioning that the term graphic novel is in general a slippery one, and may well have been taken too much for granted. Even in Stephen Weiner's *Faster Than a Speeding Bullet*, the subtitle of which is "The Rise of the Graphic Novel," the term remains quite broad, and perhaps its best definition is given in Will Eisner's introduction to the book: "Graphic novels, as I define them, are book-length comic books that are meant to be read as one story" (ix). Weiner does indicate that the term came originally from Eisner "who coined the term while trying to persuade the editors at Bantam Books to publish [a] book-length comic book" (17). Dave Sim called his collected Cerberus stories a "phone book" (27), to which Weiner responds "readers were interested in bound comic book collections, whether they were called phone books, comic book novels, albums, or graphic novels." (27). Weiner is also a little slippery with the term when he's talking about Jeff Smith's *Bone* as being a series of nine graphic novels—I'd argue that it's a single graphic novel that was broken up into nine parts until its most recent incarnation from Cartoon Books as "the complete cartoon epic in one volume." We might add that term, "cartoon epic" to the others listed above, as one more useful term that hasn't quite caught on, along with the term Seth uses on the title page of *Clyde Fans Book One*, "a picture novella"… Cf. Stephen Weiner, *Faster Than a Speeding Bullet: The Rise of the Graphic Novel* (New York: NBM, 2003).

Douglas Wolk covers similar ground on pages 43 and 60-64 of *Reading Comics* and makes at least a little more progress. Wolk prefers the use of the term "comics" and feels there there's an ideological component that's troubling to the term "graphic novel": "As a ten-dollar phrase, it implies that the graphic novel is serious in a way that the lowly comic book isn't… [T]o this day, people talk about 'graphic novels' instead of comics when they're trying to be deferential or trying to imply that they're being serious… it plays into comics culture's slightly miserable striving

So, the formal transition from thinking of *Ed* as a series of albums to thinking of *Ed* as a graphic novel is a tough one, particularly since Brown, working in a surrealism-derived mode, begins without a complete plan and allows the ending to sneak up on him. He can justify fitting the mini-comic material into the graphic novel, despite differences in drawing style and content, by relegating them to being "Introductory Pieces" and because he needs some of them. Even here, though, he finds himself making choices to trim and adapt the material. But when thinking about the definitive form of Ed, he has to make the choice of deciding if he wants something that feels like an album and a half (or one longer album and one shorter album) or something that feels like a graphic novel. Brown is smart enough to realize he can't have it both ways, and he makes a decision to commit himself to the more current notion of the form (even if he's not altogether comfortable with the name "graphic novel") even though that means he will have to dramatically revise the text as it was originally published. He does that by focusing it, by cutting off the later Ed material since it opens the door to something else.

In that sense, Brown is right to kill off the later Ed material. It's a very savvy move that makes the book feel more relevant and more contemporary. I find myself believing this despite the fact that I like certain elements of the later Ed story a great deal and, indeed, even wish they'd been developed further, that the story had been continued.

At the same time, when taken as a part of *Yummy Fur*, the Ed story has a different sort of power, and in that form, as the center for a comic book series, it works nicely. It's a shame that that experience of reading *Yummy Fur*, which was really unlike anything many of

....

for 'acknowledgement' and 'respect.'" (63-64) Then Wolk goes on to periodically use the term since it is, at times, conveniently descriptive.

In any case, "graphic novel" has become a kind of catch-all term, something that marketers seem to love, though I don't think I've met any cartoonists who are completely satisfied with it. More work needs to be done to try to define the term and make it mean something specific and critically useful.

us had ever experienced before, can't be preserved, that beside the "graphic-novel" version of Ed there isn't also published a bound version of *Yummy Fur* #1-18. There is enough room in the world for both.

I say YF#1-18 not only because that's the issue span of the Ed story; it's also because with YF#19 Brown's approach changes drastically. The longer work from then on now has an autobiographical rather than a surreal feel to it, and it comes off as more controlled and self-assured. It is also generally a great deal shorter than Ed (even than the edited version of Ed) and one gets the sense that while Brown is still trying new things and expanding his range, he's also gotten more deliberate. The primary stories in issues #19-#32 have all appeared in book form. "Helder," "Showing Helder," "Danny's Story," "The Little Man," and "Knock Knock"[11] all appeared in *The Little Man*. "Disgust" was published in book form as *The Playboy*, and "Fuck" was published as *I Never Liked You*. Unlike the Ed story, they were all reprinted in essentially the same configuration they were originally published in[12].

Most of the penultimate issue of *Yummy Fur* (YF#31) and all of the last issue (YF#32) are dedicated to *Matthew*, as if the gospels that have been occupying a secondary place to this point are now jockeying to take over the main story position. But that would be a sign that *Yummy Fur* is ending. Brown, having moved the autobiographical to the forefront, loses interest when it disappears and thus decides he needs a new name (*Underwater*) and a new idea so as to start again.

....

[11] "Knock Knock" doesn't have a title in *Yummy Fur*, but is labeled as this in the table of contents of *The Little Man*.

[12] This is true of the first book edition of *The Playboy*, but there are some substantive (albeit mostly minor) changes to the 2013 edition. In any case, the story line of *The Playboy* remains unchanged. See Chapter Four, footnote 7 for more information.

Fig. 28. *Yummy Fur* #7, 1:1.

CHAPTER FOUR
LOOSE ENDS

SMALL CHANGES

Since, I began this book by speaking about the way in which a hyphen and lack of capitalization might have a lot to tell us about *Ed the Happy Clown*, it seems to me, before concluding, worth talking about the smaller changes, the things that we hardly notice that nevertheless in fact do impact our reading experience, subtly helping to make *Ed* a different experience than *Yummy Fur*. These are small changes, but in a medium with such a large visual component, they're not insignificant. I cover each of those quickly below.

SIZE MATTERS

Various editions of *Ed* have produced Brown's artwork at various sizes (see Plate 2a and 2b)[1]. According to Brown "The artwork was reproduced at its largest in the Vortex issues of YF, at an in-between size for the mini-comic issues, and at its smallest in the D&Q printings (including the 2012 edition of the book)." For Brown, the

....
[1] Comparative view of different editions of Ed. 2012 *Ed* is top left, the mini-comic is bottom left, and the Vortex serial comic is on the right.

Fig. 29a. *Yummy Fur* #4, 3:3. Censored.

ideal size is that of the 2012 edition: "The smaller the better, as long as the words are still legible."

The 2012 edition has a larger gutter than either the mini-comic or the Vortex *Yummy Fur*, as well as more blank space around the edge of the page. The result is that a larger gap exists between one page of panels and the next, and between the pages and the edge of the book. This makes the images feel more contained and isolated.

That feeling is something, I think, augmented by two things in the 2012 hardcover edition. The first is that it's printed on archival-quality paper, which is quite white, and not likely to yellow with time, which means that the white space stays crisp and white in a way that it never was for the comic book (or, to a lesser degree, for the mini-comic). Blank space remains blank.

The second is that a hardcover edition, as I've suggested earlier, has a much different feel to it: a different heft, a different weight, a different resistance than a comic or a mini-comic. If you pick up a comic book, you know it is one in a series of comic books, part of an ongoing saga, and unless the series has already come to an end you have no way of knowing how long it might go (sometimes, as Brown himself knows, even its creator has no idea how long it might go). Your reading of any given story is interrupted from issue to issue and broken up by letters pages, advertisements, a secondary story, and so on. There's a diffusion or dispersion of energy. With a graphic novel, on the other hand, there's a sense of completeness and finality, of containment: it all exists between those two hard covers. In addition, instead of something floppy that sags in our hands or our laps as we read, we have something stiff and resistant. There's no question that such palpabilities change the sensations of the reading experience.

Speaking of size mattering, I think it's interesting that in a book that deals with penis extensions Brown insists that he wants the images to be as small as possible. It's also hard not to think that while Bick is trying to have his cock enlarged, Brown is lopping off a good part of the end of the Ed story. It's hard for me not to think of both of these things as ironic sub-verbal commentary on Brown's part.

CENSORSHIP

One of the most famous panels of *Yummy Fur* is the censored panel from *Yummy Fur* #4. His publisher Bill Marks was uncertain about whether it was a good idea to show an erect penis in the process of ejaculating, worrying that "it might get stopped at the border on the way into the U-S[2] (where most of our sales were)". Asked to redraw it in a way that "it would still be obvious that Justin was masturbating but without the ejaculating penis being visible," Brown instead decided that "if I was going to be censored I wanted my readers to know it was happening, so instead of redrawing the picture I obscured the offensive part of the panel with an explanation." (see Fig. 29a)

----

[2] Notice the hyphen. Once Brown uses it in his subtitle it begins to creep into the most unlikely places, almost as if it were trying to call attention to itself…

Fig. 29b. *Ed the Happy Clown*, 42:3. Uncensored.

The explanation offers the small expressionless bunny that Brown often uses as a stand-in for himself giving an apology: "Sorry folks but this picture of a penis ejaculating onto a hand has been censored." It also offers a replacement: "If any of you want to see the page as I originally drew it send me a self addressed envelope (and an age statement) care of Vortex Comics and I'll send you a photocopy."[3]

All later versions of the Ed story remove this panel and replace it with the uncensored version of the drawing, which is exactly as Brown describes it: Justin's penis ejaculating onto his curled hand. (see Fig. 29b) It's how the image was meant to be shown, and yet, still, something is lost. The censored image of the penis feels more shocking than the image itself. If you were reading *Yummy Fur* in order, you also had a sense that you were part of something, of a conflict with censorship. I don't know how many people actually wrote and asked for the uncensored version of the panel,[4] but the

----

[3] Quoted from the notes for the 2012 *Ed*, p 216, which also reproduces the censored version of the image.

[4] Neither does Brown, exactly. When I asked him if people wrote asking for it, he responded "Yes, quite a few. Maybe a hundred, maybe 200, I can't remember for sure."

idea that you could and thus circumvent the censors was a nice one. And the addition of "(and an age statement)", which suggested that Brown and his publisher could face the danger of prosecution, made it feel even more serious. There was a whole ethos and a whole sense of community suggested by the way that Brown handled the censorship of a single panel.

Fig. 30. *Ed the Happy Clown*, 70:1

In addition, it's one of the few moments in the Ed story where Brown breaks the frame, drawing us out of the story and into the politics of comics and comic publication. In that sense, as a moment, it has a mildly metafictional aspect that feels like the precursor of Brown's later piece "Showing Helder."

If, on the other hand, there's just the ejaculating penis, you pass over the panel quickly, almost without noticing it. The metafictional moment is lost, the breaking of the frame goes away. It just becomes a mildly challenging panel in a story in which very quickly the challenges will become far, far greater. Clearly that was what Brown originally wanted—he just wanted to tell his story without censorship. But we've lost a rallying point, a moment we anti-censorshippers can gather around.

In addition, it seems likely that this small moment of single-panel censorship had a large influence on the shape and direction of the Ed story. Rather than avoiding images likely to be censored, Brown's response for the next issue, YF#5 was exactly the opposite: he introduces an erect, liquid-vomiting penis with the head of Ronald Reagan (see Fig. 30) and draws it over and over.[5] This ends up being

---

[5] Brown says about this in his notes to the 2012 *Ed*, "I do have to wonder what

Fig. 31. *Ed the Happy Clown*, 220:1

so central to the plot and to the development of the story that there's no way really of censoring it without losing the story.

Rather than censoring the images, the inside cover (and first panel) of YF#5 offers a caution (see Fig. 31). It depicts a drafting table with a hand stabbing a knife into a worn piece of paper labeled "Warning!"[6] It explains: "While in prison (*Yummy Fur* #3) Ed contracted a disease which (as will become apparent in the pages to follow) has horribly disfigured a certain area of his body the depiction of which is so disgusting and shocking that readers with delicate dispositions (or stomachs) are advised to venture no further into this comic book!" This panel, not as relevant for the graphic novel, is not dropped exactly: it's replaced by a black panel depicting nothing. This allows for an easier transition from the murder at the end of chapter two to the events of chapter three, and also avoids breaking the frame in a way that the panel originally did.

By simultaneously offering the revised/restored version and reproducing in the notes images of both panels, Brown in a sense gets the best of both worlds: he gives us both the way he wants the two panels and the history of the way the panels used to be, as well as explanations for his changes.[7]

....

was going on in my head here. Seth believes that I'm a knee-jerk contrarian, and occasionally it does seem like he might be right." (220) In other words, telling Brown that he isn't allowed to draw an erect penis is the best way of getting him to draw erect penises.

[6] Also reproduced on page 220 of the 2012 *Ed*.

[7] Brown does this to a much greater extent in his most recent version of *The Playboy* (Montreal: Drawn & Quarterly, 2013). As he says in his notes to that book: "I've made some changes to the strip for this edition. Besides rearranging the word-balloons and rewriting many of them, I've also removed certain panels that appeared in previous versions of *The Playboy*. But don't worry, you're not missing any of the artwork; I'm printing all of the deleted panels in this notes section." (205) Perhaps Brown chooses to do this here because the story itself has the same shape, approximate length, and ending in each edition. For *Ed the Happy Clown*, he does reproduce a number of panels in the notes pages from within issues 1-12 of *Yummy Fur*, documenting changes, but "None of the Ed material from Y-F #13 to Y-F #16

The cover of YF#5 also alludes to censorship (see Plate 3). It shows the Chester Brown bunny standing in the middle of a purple-and-blue bullseye painted on the ground with the words "Adults Only" painted in the center of it. Two shell craters mar the bullseye, and the bunny is pleading "Don't Shoot!" This image isn't included in the 2012 Ed, either in the text proper or in the notes.

That Brown continued, however, to think about censorship issues as he wrote *Yummy Fur*—and how could he help it, considering the sorts of things he was drawing for the Ed story?—is shown by his writing a piece on the inside back cover of YF#9 against proposed Canadian anti-pornography legislation.

SHIFTS IN PANELING

Since, as already mentioned, Brown draws in individual panels rather than pages, he has less compunction than most cartoonists about shifting the positioning of panels on his pages. I've spoken a little bit about this already, but it's worth exploring at least one other example. I'll also mention, in passing, that these shifts are something that happen a lot in the transition from *Yummy Fur* to *Ed*, and though they often don't seem terribly significant, sometimes they really do make a difference. Whether you see something at the end of a page or the first thing when you turn the page over has an effect on how you anticipate what's on the next page, what follows, etc. The largest transition we experience as we're reading comes in turning the page. It's a brief moment, just as long as it takes for our fingers to flip the page over and our eyes to go to the top, but it's much less brief than the time it takes for our eye to flick from the bottom of an even-numbered page across the gutter and to the top

....

appears in this book." (241) Not even in the notes.

  It's also interesting what he chooses not to correct in *The Playboy*. On page 113, for instance, he mentions in his notes that he forgot to draw the centerfold depicted, but he doesn't bother to draw it in retroactively, just acknowledging that he didn't do it. Why preserve that while changing the other things he mentions?

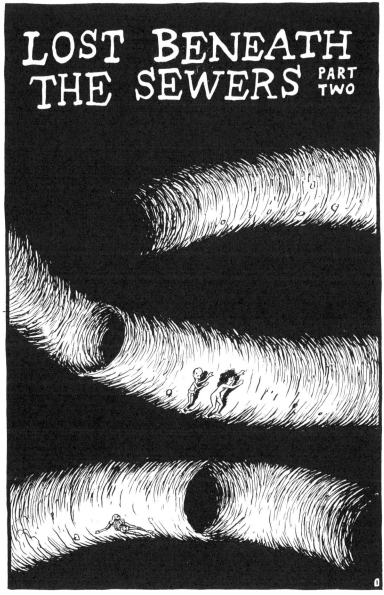

Fig. 32a. *Yummy Fur #8*, 1:1

of the odd-numbered one that follows it. And even briefer is the rapid movement of the eye from panel to panel as we transform the static images into a progression.

The way we as readers make sense of a text is by thinking of it as a series of meaning blocks, using smaller blocks to build up larger units of meaning. In a comic, we use parts of a panel, both visual and verbal, to build up a panel. Then we use the panel to build up a page. Simultaneously, we use a series of panels (and full or partial pages) to build up a scene. Then a series of scenes to build a story. Then a series of pages of perhaps simultaneously running stories to build an issue. Then a series of issues to build a larger narrative. We're often thinking of an issue as having a contained structure, which is why cartoonists, including Brown, sometimes feel compelled to label a new issue as a continuation of a story or finish an issue with the words "continued next issue." So, different ways of thinking about these building blocks sometimes jostle against one another. With a graphic novel, the first building blocks are the same, but instead of building issues out of several simultaneously running stories we build chapters up to a larger narrative. But the way we build those chapters is the same as in comic books: with panels assembled in pages. And as the arrangements of these panels or pages shift, the shape of the larger structures of meaning can skew or shift as well.

In the move of the Ed material from YF#8 to chapter six of the 2012 *Ed the Happy Clown* this shift in paneling happens. In YF#8, the issue begins with a single full-page panel (see Fig. 32a), titled "Lost Beneath the Sewers Part Two." It shows three seemingly unconnected tunnels passing through darkness. The top one is empty, the middle one shows Ed and Josie, the bottom one shows skeletal remains. In the 2012 *Ed*, this panel is reduced to a quarter of a page (one double-length panel) and just features a portion of the middle tunnel (see Fig. 32b). As a result, the last two panels on the page are forced onto the next page, and this is the case for the entire chapter. In other words, except for the first page, the bottom two panels of each page in *Yummy Fur* become the top two panels

Fig. 32b Same Panel, 112:1 in *Ed the Happy Clown*

of each page in *Ed*.

One reason Brown might allow this is because the Ed story in YF#8 ends 3/4ths of the way down the page, with the last ¼ page used to give the contents of the next issue: "The Awful Secret of the Micro-Dimension." By shifting the panels in this way, Brown gets the graphic novel chapter to come out evenly, to end at the end of the page.

At the same time, it does change the rhythm of the story and causes shifts in emphasis. Some serve the work well, others perhaps do not.

For instance, the second page of the *Yummy Fur* version ends dramatically with Josie being shot without our having seen who has shot her. This allows the third page to begin with a panel showing Josie's apparently dead corpse. That page will end with the corpse as well, this time as part of a larger tableau with the mother-and-daughter pygmy hunters shining a flashlight on the body. While the equivalent pages in the graphic novel (pages 112-113) do lose the surprise of having the page break right after Josie has been shot, page 113 does begin with the flash and noise of bullets being fired (113:1) and ends with a hand holding a smoking gun (113:8), giving the page a nice formal unity. And page 114 ends with a gun going off and us not knowing whether Ed has been shot, which is a more satisfying way to end that page than the way YF ends it: there the final panel is the daughter talking to the mother after having tackled her, telling her that they can't kill Ed.

On an aesthetic level, in the YF version it allows the eighth page, as Ed is bleeding in the tunnel, to have all dark backgrounds, and the ninth page, after the borer has arrived, to have lighter backgrounds, which is aesthetically pleasing in a way that those pages in the 2012 *Ed* are not.

So, something gained, something lost. It's difficult to say definitively that the page sequencing in one version is better than the other. But it's easy to see, here and elsewhere, that it's different. That difference has a quiet, almost subconscious, effect on the reading experience.

COVERS VS. CHAPTER COVERS

Both the mini-comic and the serial comic of *Yummy Fur* have, necessarily, covers. As I've mentioned, the first issues of the serial comic also published the covers of the mini-comic, ending up, with a few small exceptions, replicating the order and sequence: it's as if you open up the first issue of the serial comic and find instead that you've bought three mini-comics. Then, in addition, each Vortex *Yummy Fur* issue has its own cover, which serves as an opportunity or an occasion to entice or direct the reader.

By the time you get to the book version, that's changed. In the move away from presenting the whole mini-comic to just giving selected "Introductory Pieces" the reproductions of the mini-comics covers have largely dropped out.

"Introductory Pieces" uses the title page of mini-comic #5 as its chapter cover page.

Chapter one uses an image from the cover of mini-comic #7, which is also the cover of YF#3. This "cover" is only half size, and "Adventures in Science" begins later on the same page.

Chapter two uses an image that is not from a *Yummy Fur* cover but is instead a variation of the Madonna and child image that appears in panels 4-6 of page 45. In his notes to *Ed the Happy Clown* Brown explains where it came from: "In 1988, Vortex wrapped sets of the first four Vortex issues of YUMMY FUR in clear plastic to sell to people who had missed the early issues. This drawing was printed on a separate piece of paper and slipped into the front of the package as a new cover." (215)

Chapter three is a 2/3rds of a page "cover" and is simply black space—it's a replacement for the warning/caution that Brown had originally included as the first panel inside the issue (see the censorship sub-chapter).

Chapter four is an image from the television of a devil staring at the world and saying "But who wants it?" and also is not a *Yummy Fur* cover. Brown describes it as "an homage to Steve Gerber" (221). It appears in uncropped form and with a few small additions in YF#6 as the first page, a kind of inner title page.

Chapter five does something similar, using the first panel of YF#7 as its title page (it occupies the top 2/3rds of the page) though this image is less cropped than it is in *Yummy Fur*. There's an interesting change here: text within an arrow pointing to the man originally said "This character died back in *Yummy Fur #3* so don't pay any attention to him." (see Fig. 27) In the graphic novel version "*Yummy Fur #3*" is emended to "Chapter One".

Chapter six uses the cover of *Yummy Fur* #8.

In an interesting twist, chapter seven moves backwards, using the cover of *Yummy Fur* #7, in smaller form, as if taking a picture of a separate comic book. Since YF#7 was done as if it were a comic book called "Adventures in Science" with the words "Yummy Fur" written over it (See Plate 4), Brown reproduces, in black and white form, the entire cover, except for the words "Yummy Fur", at an angle against a black background.

Chapter eight uses the first panel of YF#10 as its chapter page, blotting out the words "Destroy All Vampires" and writing instead "Chapter Eight". This image occupies about half the page.

Chapter nine uses the background of the cover of YF#11, without the images laid on top of it. On YF#11 this appears as a yellowish stream of liquid, perhaps urine oozing down a wall. In the 2012 *Ed*, since it's black-and-white it's difficult to tell what fluid it is exactly. A white rectangle containing this image is framed against a black background. On YF#11, over the top of the fluid is a large squarish blue rectangle containing the magazine name and other information and an angled longer rectangle depicting Chet and Josie kissing.

Chapter ten uses a full-page chapter cover image based on the second frame of YF#17 depicting a running pygmy. It's a different image, much expanded, wordless (a speech bubble depicts the pygmy's rapid breathing in the original and the splashing of his feet are also verbally marked), and with a shadow in the background that clearly shows he is being pursued.

Chapter eleven begins with a new image, a scalpel against a black background that occupies about half the page. In YF#12 this place is occupied by the words "Going Home".

Chapter twelve is the only chapter beginning to occupy merely a single normal-sized panel (1/6th of the page). By doing this, Brown ends up shifting the paneling just a little bit so that all the panels on pages 201-203 are new. This chapter "cover" panel is of flames and prefigures the fires of hell we'll get a few pages later.

With the exceptions of the chapters that didn't exist when it was published (chapters 10 and 12), the 1989 edition of Ed contains all these chapter headings just as they are here in the 2012 edition.

In short, Brown uses different title page strategies from chapter to chapter, sometimes offering a full page for transition at other times only a small panel. There's a kind of makeshift bricolage going on which pays tribute to some of the original comic covers but often as not modifies them, changes them, and offers other things in their place. Brown seems to want to regularize *Ed* in its definitive version and yet he simultaneously leaves a strange amount of randomness and play, evidence of Ed's past incarnation in *Yummy Fur*. Even in something as simple as the way Brown moves from chapter to chapter we can see this double impulse.

&

There are, of course, many more things that could be discussed, and individual manifestations of the generalities I've already mentioned could certainly be discussed in more detail. But the purpose of this book is not to be an exhaustive textual study: it is less to catalog all the changes existing between different tellings of the Ed story and more to give a sense of the different impulses behind *Yummy Fur* and the consolidation of *Ed the Happy Clown* later as a book, and through it to learn something about how to use choices, both small and large, to build significant effects that support whatever genre one is operating in. These effects and shifts are clearer in *Ed/Yummy Fur* than in almost any other story, and this, I feel, is one reason, among many, why *Ed/Yummy Fur* will continue to be important in the history of the development of comics as an art form.

Fig. 33. *Yummy Fur #1*, 12:1

CONCLUSION

Sometimes, when I'm reading an old superhero comic from the 50s or 60s I find myself imagining a new story into the images, reconsidering the sometimes-tired formulas of writers who know the constraints of their genre and medium almost too well and adhere unflinchingly to them. It's not that I don't admire a great deal about those comics, only that, as I look at them more and more closely, I begin to see them as containing a myriad of unfulfilled possibilities. I've gone so far with some of the early *Strange Adventures* appearances of Deadman that Neal Adams drew as to write a good chunk of a new script, trying to find the other stories hiding in the progression of images making up a less than scintillating narrative.

Part of Grant Morrison's career was built on a similar sort of gesture: taking DC or Marvel figures that we thought we knew, like the X-Men or Superman, or comics we might have heard of but probably mostly never really read (like *Animal Man* or *Doom Patrol*), and writing them in a way that took the formulas of the genre progressively apart—not just to deconstruct the superhero myth, but to provide, in addition, something new. Same with Alan Moore and his approach to *Swamp Thing*: Moore takes the premise of the original swamp thing as a mutated man and replaces him with something that was never human at all. Or his *Watchmen*, which rewrites less a specific hero and more the notions of an entire genre.

I would argue that Brown's *Ed the Happy Clown* should be considered in similar terms. But that instead of rewriting somebody else's work or instead of picking up a character we're already familiar with, he takes his own story, the Ed story as presented in *Yummy Fur*, and reworks that. In fact, even the development of Ed within *Yummy Fur* might be thought of as a series of revisions and shifts. Some of these are formal and based on the constraints of a mini-comic vs. a comic vs. a graphic novel— these sorts of revisions were occurring at each stage of writing *Yummy Fur*, and culminate in *Ed*. Others are at least partly story revisions or shifts taking place just for the graphic novel: the decision to cut a good chunk of the ending and move the remaining material forward, the decision to write a new ending, the decision to leave Christian's origins unexplained, etc. But even these sorts of revisions are occurring at every step of the composition process as well: Brown will write and draw, for instance, Josie's murder scene and a few issues later he will circle back to it from a different perspective, returning to the scene in such a way as to let us see that while Josie was being murdered Ed was lying beaten up in the bushes nearby. This is a revision of what was originally there, a way of bringing a connection in after the fact, as Brown himself has admitted.[1] *Yummy Fur*, then, was a series being constantly revised on the fly, and *Ed the Happy Clown* is the culmination of that revision.[2]

....

[1] From his interview with Scott Grammel: "When I first did issue #4 I didn't know that Ed was in the bushes a couple feet away. So yeah, I'm adding and changing as I go along. As much as I can." Brown's phrasing is interesting here: it's not that he changed things to insert Ed in the bushes but that he "didn't know" Ed was in the bushes. Brown speaks as if he had discovered a fact rather than invented something that changes his story.

[2] This may help to explain why Brown feels "happy" with the idea that *Yummy Fur* might disappear: essentially *Yummy Fur* can be read as a forum for drafting work, with the final definitive versions coming out only later. That's most obvious with *Ed*, since it's the most substantially revised, but it's remarkable to realize a) how many of the projects that Brown went on to collect in book form first originated in *Yummy Fur* and b) how several projects begun there (the gospels) were never finished. As he showed with *Underwater* and with the gospels (which were done both in *Yummy Fur* and *Underwater*), Brown isn't afraid to either abandon or dramatically revise a project he works on in serial comic book form.

Brown revises himself publically, and does so more radically than any other comic artist I am aware of. And, as with successive revisions and justifications of a character like Swamp Thing by different writers ("he's a man, no he's a plant, wait it's all explained by there having been many different swamp things, no wait now he's a man again—just suspend your disbelief and go with whatever we say through this new series"), there are often threads of earlier notions and ideas that continue to persist, little bits and pieces of ideas abandoned or not followed through. But one of the interesting things about this for Brown's readers and his fellow artists is that we're being given a window into how a creative mind works. Looking at *Yummy Fur* and *Ed the Happy Clown* together, we're seeing in public the processing and exploration that usually occurs in sketchbooks or only in the mind, and learning as a result how intuitive and forced leaps are often made on the way to writing what seems in the end a unified book.

What is the relationship of the artist to his past production? There is no clear answer to this; indeed, it seems different for every artist. Some people fetishize the things they've already done, others think of it almost as if they were written by another person. Some people want to forget it, other people want to revise and rearrange it.

Brown (at least in relation to *Ed the Happy Clown*) seems to be of that latter camp, and even with his other works that remain relatively intact in the transition from comic book to book he extensively contexts and annotates.[3] He's in good company: Henry James revised his second novel, *Roderick Hudson*, four different times at different points in his life, and all of these versions were published. His last revision was done more than 30 years after the novel was first published and made it a radically different creature, something that the older James felt represented him and his views better than the earlier version written when he was young.

....

[3] For instance, when Brown moved from the comic form of *Louis Riel* to the book form, he substantially redrew it: "For the book version, I redrew Riel in almost every panel for the first 79 pages. There were other minor changes."

There's an element of this in Brown's revisions as well, as Brown has acknowledged in particular about *Ed*'s rewritten ending: it better suits his sense of how things should be.

When people are at the beginning of their artistic production, they often don't quite know what they're doing and, as a result, extraordinary things can happen (though epic failures can occur as well—luckily, though, there's not nearly as large an audience for them as for the epic failures that can come later). The same is the case early in a genre: as we're feeling our way, we often strike out in unexpected directions, and things that seem obvious later can't even be imagined at the time. Franco Moretti speaks of this in regard to clues and the 19th century detective story: it took a while for the idea that the *clue* was essential to detective fiction to develop, and even a good many of the Sherlock Holmes stories don't really have clues *per se*. A writer of detective fiction might use clues in one story and then not in the next. "They found them by chance, and never really understood *what* they had found." (215)[4] But, Moretti points out, Doyle did develop something else entirely different: the mythical almost superhuman qualities of the detective that typifies Holmes and which, much more than clues, is what we cling to. Once we get to the point where the genre people know that detective stories have clues, that clues are *essential*, we need something else to distinguish between a good detective story and a bad one. That ends up being the quirks or the personality of the detective, something that Doyle had understood from the beginning, and the reason that Sherlock Holmes has had a better shelf-life than any other detective.

One of the real strengths of *Yummy Fur* is that, especially in the early issues, it doesn't know what it's doing. And as it shifts its notion of what it thinks it is doing, both formally and aesthetically, different possibilities open up. I'm reminded of Dashiell Hammett's *Red Harvest*, which was written on the cusp of the development of a genre, the hard-boiled genre. Very soon afterward, with Raymond Chandler, much about the

....

[4] Franco Moretti, "The Slaughterhouse of Literature" *Modern Language Quarterly* 61:1 (March 2000): 207-227.

genre would become formalized and figured out: we'd be able to see its characteristics with greater clarity. We don't see that in Hammett, who is writing his way, quite literally, into unchartered territory, trying to find an entirely new place for detective fiction to go. Reading *Red Harvest*, you get the sense, abruptly, that anything can happen. And you get the sense that Hammett too is realizing this as he's writing, just as you are when you're reading. It's not as smooth and comfortable a ride as a Chandler novel, but it may be, in many respects, a more exciting one because someone has cut the brake lines—and you get the sense that it might be Hammett who has cut them. I feel the same way about *Yummy Fur*. That randomness and exuberance is both *Yummy Fur*'s strength and its weakness. *Ed the Happy Clown* both gives that sensation and also gives a sense, in the way it shapes itself after the fact, that Brown is in fact in control of the car after all.

The later, definitive version of *Ed the Happy Clown* is itself a creative act that shifts and redirects the original creative act and energy that was *Yummy Fur*. Without thinking about the two side-by-side, this is quite difficult to see fully, let alone appreciate. In writing the definitive version of *Ed the Happy Clown*, Brown undertook the very difficult task of revisiting old work—work written when he and his aesthetic were different than they were to become—and reshaping it not enough to bring it in line with his then-current aesthetic practice but only enough that it becomes a bridge between his past material and the material to come. By so doing he puts it to rest. In the process, all sorts of things are changed, omitted, or lost, some minor and others major, and Brown himself approaches the task seemingly ruthlessly, hoping that the old version of Ed, in his own words, will be forgotten. At the same time there's still a remainder or supplement in the revised text, pointing to the material that once was there: little strange moments that we are no longer quite sure what to do with. And, ultimately, I'd argue that an understanding of Brown's skill as an artist and a creator really hinges on an understanding of the way he engages in the art of sublime subtraction, of distillation, as he pillages *Yummy Fur* to create for us his definitive version of *Ed the Happy Clown*.

APPENDIX

INTERVIEW WITH CHESTER BROWN

Brian Evenson: Many of the projects that you later collected as graphic novels or as book-length projects started in *Yummy Fur*— for instance, *Ed the Happy Clown*, *I Never Liked You*, *The Playboy*. Was there a moment in writing Ed that you realized that it was a book in its own right? Was that something that happened gradually? When in the process of writing did it happen?

Chester Brown: I realized pretty early on when I was serializing the story in the Vortex issues of YF that we'd probably be reprinting the episodes in book form. I didn't think there would be only one book — I was assuming I would continue with the character and his world for a long time (maybe the rest of my life) and that there would be a series of Ed books. With the Ed installments in YF 13 and beyond I began to feel dissatisfied — that I'd exhausted the material and it was time to move on. When I wrapped up the series in YF 18, it didn't seem like there was enough good material for a second book, so that's when it became evident that there would only be the one book.

Have you found yourself thinking about the book form of a story while you're still working on the comic book version?

It would depend on the project. By the time I was working on *I Never Liked You*, I was much more focused on how the story would work as a graphic novel than in how the serialized episodes would read individually.

Do you feel that the comic book demands different things?

I don't know how to answer this question.

Is the comic book now for you a stage on the way to a final, book version? Does it feel transitional?

No, I didn't serialize *Paying For It*, and I don't intend to go back to serialization.

I don't think it's until the 2012 edition that you call *Ed the Happy Clown* a graphic novel on the cover. Before that it's called *A Yummy Fur Book* and *The Definitive Ed Book*. What made you decide to call it a graphic novel?

I've never been happy with the term graphic novel. It's too obviously an attempt to sound respectable. But it's caught on now, for whatever reason, so there's not much use in fighting it.

With the *Yummy Fur* material that would become *I Never Liked You* and *The Playboy*, did you have more of a sense from the beginning of each project that you were writing books?

I didn't think of *The Playboy* as a book when I began it. I didn't plan out the first installment in YF 21 — I just started writing and drawing, seeing where my memories would take me. I had no idea how long it might be, I thought I might be able to wrap it up in one issue. I did plan out *I Never Liked You* to some degree, and I realized that it would be longer than an issue. I probably was thinking of it abstractly as a book, but I was much more concerned with filling issues of YF at that time.

You call the book version of *I Never Liked You* a "comic-strip narrative" and the 1992 version of *The Playboy* a "comic book". Did you see them as different forms or are those different names

for the same thing?

They're not synonyms, but a comic book can contain a comic-strip narrative, and a comic-strip narrative can be in a comic book.

The 2013 version of *The Playboy* changes the subtitle to a "comic-strip memoir". What made you decide to make that change?

Originally the cover read, The Playboy: A Comic Book. It seems to me that the term "comic book" is on the way out.

Much of *Yummy Fur* was collected into books, but much hasn't been: the gospel stories, for instance, or the last few installments of the Ed story that you chose to leave out of the finished *Ed* book. Were you thinking of the floppy single-issue comic as a testing ground?

Not at the beginning. Maybe by the time of *Underwater* I was starting to think that way.

Is part of the reason for not collecting certain material later just the speed with which those early single issues had to be done? Did you feel that you'd taken a few false steps that you wanted to correct or was it a matter of shaping the work from a more objective position once you had some time and distance or…?

The material that was reprinted was, for the most part, the material I liked better. I didn't like my gospel adaptations, I didn't like the later Ed installments.

With the rise of graphic novels, it seems likely that *Ed the Happy Clown* will be remembered primary by the definitive version, which leaves off the last few episodes. How do you feel knowing that the *Yummy Fur* version might be lost to most readers?

Happy.

Do you ever regret the amount of work you spent on those later Ed episodes?

My regrets are fleeting and of-the-moment. I finished Ed over twenty years ago. I have no regrets that go back that far in time.

Are there parts of those later Ed pages (YF 13-18) that you remain fond of even if you're happy for the whole of it to be lost?

Nope.

You've talked in interviews about your style being to draw a single panel. Has that always been the case, even in the early mini-comic of *Yummy Fur*?

Yes, I first did it with "Walrus Blubber Sandwich" in 1981, which pre-dates the first Ed strip.

How does that composition choice make you think about things differently? Do you feel like the idea of a page is less definite for you than other comic artists? Do you think of the page as a central unit? Or the panel? Or the book? Or…?

Unlike most narrative print cartoonists, I **never** think about the page as a whole when I'm drawing. I think either about the individual panel or how it will work in a scene, but never about the page because I won't know which panels will go on which pages until I've finished everything and I'm assembling the work for publication. I guess I think of each scene as a central unit.

One thing that interests me about the move from serial publication in floppies to book publication is that it's not unlike what happened with novels in the 19th century that were serialized in magazines and then later printed in books. Sometimes you can see the residue of the earlier format. Looking back over *Ed*, are there things that were done for later issues that don't make as much sense to you now that the definitive version stops earlier?

I don't think enough about that later material to have a real answer to this question.

Do you think with the move away from single-issue comics that the kinds of pieces that were being written to fill white space, but that still might have value, are no longer being written?

There really wasn't much "filler" stuff in YF. The continuing gospel adaptations gave me a lot of latitude from the perspective of filling the issue. The question for a particular issue might be whether it would have a one- or two-page letters section.

Has a major idea for you ever come out/started with "filler"?

I can't think of one.

The format size between the Vortex *Yummy Fur* and the 2012 *Ed the Happy Clown* is somewhat different, with the panels in the later version being about 30% smaller. Do you feel that one size is the "right" size? Or doesn't it matter as much?

I like the size of the 2012 edition best. The smaller the better, as long as the words are still legible.

What sort of size were the panels in the mini-comic? Bigger or smaller than *Yummy Fur*?

The artwork was reproduced at its largest in the Vortex issues of YF, at an in-between size for the mini-comic issues, and at its smallest in the D&Q printings (including the 2012 edition of the book).

How did things change generally, moving from one form to the other—from mini-comic to single issue floppies to graphic novel?

The big change was moving from self-published mini-comics to Vortex. It went from being a hobby to being something I was trying to making a living at (although those Vortex years were financially precarious). There's a higher level of craft in the minis than in the Vortex issues. In the Vortex period I was working so quickly.

One thing that's very interesting to me is the way that *Ed* spans several different modes of comics, and in fact several different eras. It started as a mini-comic, moved to floppies, ended with a graphic novel. That seems to reflect shifts in the industry as a whole. How do you feel about the way the comics industry has changed since you first wrote the mini-comics?

I think it's unfortunate that the comic-shop distribution system fell apart (or at least shrank drastically) but it's also the best time for the medium now — there are so many exciting young cartoonists doing great work at this point in time. The only worry is what the fate of print will be.

Issue #1- #3 of *Yummy Fur* presents itself as a kind of artifact of the mini-comic, reproducing them entirely. Did you find yourself changing a lot in terms of layout, etc., as you moved to the new form?

I began to letter the word-balloons at a smaller size, and, as I rushed to keep on a bi-monthly schedule, the level of craft dropped a bit. That's all I can think of from a form perspective.

Did you ever have regrets about using the same name (*Yummy Fur*) for the mini-comic and the comic? Has that caused some confusion over the years?

It's probably caused a little bit of confusion, but not so much that I regret holding on to that name.

Did you realize from the beginning (the first Ed appearance) that Ed would be a reoccurring character? Or did that come later?

No, I initially had no intention of drawing Ed again after doing the first six-page strip. When that strip was printed in the second

Yummy Fur mini-comic, I got some positive feedback about the character. It was at that point that I decided to at least feature him in a second strip.

When did you realize that "The Man Who Couldn't Stop" was part of the Ed story?

The Man Who Couldn't Stop was intended to be part of the Ed story right from the beginning.

In issue #1 you have "The Toilet Paper Revolt" and in issue #2, you have "Catlick Creek" about water and septic tanks. Do you see those as a precursor to your "interest" in shit in "The Man Who Couldn't Stop"?

I haven't given it any thought before now, but I can see how someone could make that connection.

Did you get to issue #3 and feel like you needed a third story in a similar space?

No. **All** of the material in the first three Vortex issues originally appeared in the YF mini-comics (including **all** of the comics in the third Vortex issue). I wouldn't have been thinking about the arrangement of the first three Vortex issues when I was putting together the minis because I didn't yet know that Vortex would be reprinting them. There was no scatological material in the fifth and sixth YF mini.

I got the impression that "City Swine" could have been the start of a longer piece. Did you ever intend to continue that?

Nope.

Same with "Walrus Blubber Sandwich", which ends pretty abruptly. Were there ever plans to make that longer?

Yes, I originally wrote a twenty page script for that strip, but I didn't have the stamina to finish it, so I had the saucer crash on the third page. Doing longer strips takes focus. I had to learn how to focus like that.

Is it just a coincidence that the short pieces you leave out of *The Little Man* are all from the mini-comic YF #4? Was that a particularly tough issue for you to put together?

I was running out of good material by that point. With the fifth issue I had to actually draw something new.

In issue #3, I think "I Live in a Bottomless Pit" is the first overtly religious installment in *Yummy Fur*, involving the Anti-Christ. Is it more than a coincidence that you move from the Anti-Christ in this issue to the Gospels in issue #4?

It wasn't planned that way. I began to get seriously interested in religion in 1983, so much of my work after that date reflects that continuing interest.

In the introduction to *The Little Man* you say: "Some of my early short strips, which were at first intended to stand complete at a few pages, were later incorporated into the long serial 'Ed the Happy Clown'". When you wrote *Yummy Fur* were you already thinking of the "Adventures in Science" pieces as being part of Ed, or did that develop only later?

The early Adventures In Science pieces were not intended to connect to Ed's story.

Why did you choose to leave pieces like "Catlick Creek", "The Eyelid Burial" and "Fire with Fire" out of *The Little Man*? Did they fall under the category that you call, in the intro to that book, "strips that feel to me now like they were collaborations, even if technically they weren't"?

Catlick Creek and The Eyelid Burial felt like collaborations, and

Fire With Fire was drawn before I moved to Toronto.

I feel that by Vortex issue #4 things have clarified for you about what you're doing. Rather than a lot of short strips we're beginning to see how things are related, and there's interest in telling a continuing story with Ed (and with the Gospels too). Do you feel that the floppy encouraged that continuity in a way that the mini-comic didn't?

It was at that point that I had to get serious about what I was doing. In December of 1986 I quit my day-job and, at the beginning of 1987, I began writing and drawing the fourth Vortex YF. I knew I'd have to produce quickly to put out six issues a year, so I decided that continuing stories made sense, rather than beginning something new each issue. It wasn't the floppy format that pushed me to do continuing stories, it was the need to produce relatively quickly.

Issue #4 for me is one of the few issues of comics I remember being really shocked by. I think it was less because of the sex and murder at the end of the Ed material in that issue and more because we go straight from that to an adaptation of the Biblical book of Mark. Do you remember why you decided to start doing the Gospels? Was it inspired by the Saints' Lives material in the *Ed* story? Despite *Yummy Fur*'s absurd strangeness, I think it's one of the last things your readers would expect.

I was obsessed with the Jesus story (and still am) — it made sense to adapt the gospels to dive into them more deeply. I had decided to start adapting Mark in YF before the Saint Justin idea came to me.

What made you decide to start with Mark rather than one of the other gospels? Was it initially something done just to fill pages, or was it something you'd thought about doing for a while?

Most Biblical scholars believe that Mark was the first of the canonical gospels. It was partly a time-saving decision: it would be material I wouldn't have to write, so I thought I could do those pages more quickly. I'm not sure if doing the gospel pages actually did take less time than the Ed pages — as half-assed as my research was, it still took some time.

I read the gospel material, particularly in the early issues, as being told straight and respectfully. They're not anti-religious or parodic. At the same time, I don't find them particularly pro-religious: Jesus seems angry and harsh a lot of the time, and there's an element of aggression running through them. Did you know what you wanted to do with them going in or did you figure it out gradually? How hard was it to manage that balance?

I wanted to do a straightforward adaptation — you're right that they weren't supposed to be anti-religious or parodic. I was surprised at how often Jesus was described as being angry in Mark. So in Matthew I deliberately gave him an angry look and then found, while doing the adaptation, that he's not as angry in that gospel.

Do you feel that the purpose behind telling the gospel stories changed as you continued to write them?

No. My fascination with the material stayed constant.

What made you decide to replicate the mini-comic covers and all in the first few issues? Why not the material but not the covers?

My original contract with Vortex was to reprint the mini-comic material in three 24-page comic-books — that's 72 pages. Everything fit almost exactly in those 72 pages.

In issue #4 of *Yummy Fur*, you don't reproduce the cover of mini-comic YF #7 within the comic itself, as you'd done with the first six issues. Instead, you use it as the cover for the issue itself— though we don't know that it's also the cover for #7 until, on the inside back cover, you reproduce it as it was in the mini-comic. You also explain there that the issue is a combination of a couple of pieces from *Yummy Fur* (mini) #6 and #7. Do you remember

what made you decide not to reproduce the cover between where #6 ended and #7 started?

I didn't have the room. The issue only contained 24 pages.

In Issue #4, you don't number the pages of the Mark story, though you number the Ed story. Did you not number those early pages for some reason? By the time we get to Issue #5, you restart the numbering each time you do Ed-related material, but continue the numbering of Mark from issue #5 on. Were you seeing Mark as a more continuous story than Ed? Why this difference?

That's something I'd forgotten about. Your guess is as good as mine.

The Saint Justin that I know about didn't lose a hand, but was a writer/theologian who wrote against the heretics and was later beheaded. Is your Saint Justin based on another actual saint or is he imaginary?

Imaginary.

Was there any reason why you chose the name Justin for your imagined saint?

If there was one, I've forgotten it.

When the panel showing Justin's ejaculating penis was censored, you offered readers a photocopy of it if they wrote to you and asked for one. Did you get many readers writing?

Yes, quite a few. Maybe a hundred, maybe 200, I can't remember for sure.

In Issue #6, you place the "Fur Bag" letters page between Ed and the Gospel of Mark, so it kind of separates the issue into two issues. Why did you decide to do this? Was it a way of creating a border between the two? What made you decide not to continue

doing that?

Again, any answer I give would be a guess. Perhaps I wanted to feature the letters page prominently in the sixth issue since none of the previous issues had one.

In Issue #7, we find the "Fur Bag" at the beginning. What made you decide to do that? It feels a little like you're playing with the structure of the comic, trying to decide what should go where… (But it can also be read as providing another border between the Mark material at the end of #6 and the Ed stuff at the start of #7.)

That's surprising. I think I tended to put the letters page at the end of the issue. Perhaps I told Bill Marks to put the page on the inside-back-cover and he made a mistake.

I'm curious about whether you feel that the story of the Demons and the Swine, told in the Mark portion of #7 has any relation to the "City Swine" piece found in issue #1.

There was no conscious connection there. "City Swine" was inspired by an incident in Gogol's "The Nose."

The 2012 version of the Ed material found in issue #8 has a slightly different rearrangement: it kicks everything down a panel for the whole of chapter six. What made you decide to do that? Does it really change the relationship of the parts to the page? Or do you tend to think more in panels than in pages?

I wanted to eliminate the "next issue" tier on page 12 of YF 8. Also, the splash panel for that issue isn't that interesting — it didn't matter if most of it disappeared.

The two pages of the "Fur Bag" in issue 8 ends up giving notes on Mark. I see this as the genesis of something I've come to think of as characteristic of your work: the way you annotate the work in complex and interesting ways.

Is that where it starts?

In issue #9 inside the back cover, you have a piece about proposed anti-pornography legislation Bill C-54. Were you starting to see the comic as a place that could be a forum for ideas (something I'd argue is the case with *Louis Riel* and *Paying For It*)?

That piece of legislation concerned me and I had a platform, so I figured, why not use it?

The Ed material from #13-18 is mostly left out of the final version (except for some things in #17). Can you talk about your reasons for doing this? I think even with the first collected book you had the notion that there might be a second volume, no? Do you feel that this Ed material just went the wrong direction? Did it shift the focus too much from what you decided you wanted the Ed book to do?

The story came to a natural end with the twelfth issue. I was keeping the story artificially alive past that point.

How do you feel about the fact that there are several versions of Ed out there? Is that simply part of the process of the way it was written? If you had a choice to go back, would you not have written the later Ed material that you didn't end up including? Or can we think of *Yummy Fur* as a kind of laboratory in which you were trying things out?

It's not emotionally upsetting that there are multiple endings to the story, but, sure, if I could go back in time, I'd do it right the first time. Not that I'm eager to go back in time. And, yes, YF was a kind of laboratory.

The later Ed material becomes quite interested, I think, in notions of doubling and identity and even of twins (Ed's masquerading as Bick, the suggestion that Ed and his "wife" might be twins). That's in the earlier Ed material too, though not

quite as strongly. Do you have a sense of where that interest was coming from?

Nope.

I'm interested in the cover of #15 which says "1st issue! Ha ha! Just Kidding! Actually it's the Fifteenth Issue." What made you decide to do that? Was it because it was the first issue of the book of Matthew?

It was just a joke. I was imagining that there was someone out there who was searching for the first issue and would be momentarily fooled into thinking they'd found it.

How do you think things shifted for you in moving from the book of Mark to the book of Matthew? Was anything changing?

I used very few narrative captions in Matthew, whereas almost every panel in Mark has one. I planned to switch away from narrative captions for Matthew when I began Mark.

The Matthew material in #15 starts in the middle of the page, and you don't number it separately from the other material as you did with the book of Mark. Why not? Were you seeing the book as more integrated as a whole? (I know it's a very small thing I'm asking, but I think small things can reveal a lot.)

I'm guessing I got to panel 12:2, realized it was a good panel to end that Ed installment, and figured, why not start Matthew here instead of coming up with space-filler for the rest of the page? And, since Matthew started half-way through the page, it didn't make sense to number it separately.

Some of the Ed material in #17 makes it into the Ed books. This is by far the most significant rearrangement/insertion of material. Did you have any difficulties trying to make it fit with the gap there? Or do you feel that the material you wrote in 13-

16 that you left out helped you to get to this material, which was what was really needed?

No, it seemed pretty obvious what I could use from YF 17 for the second edition of the book. There was no difficulty.

I'm curious, too, about the material on pages 12-15 of issue #17, in which Josie is on fire, put out by her mother and boyfriend and then carried outside, put in the sun, catches flame, goes down into the sewers. That's one of the few moments where for the books you not only leave *Yummy Fur* Ed material out, but draw new material. What made you decide to do that?

Josie's heroic end in YF 18 seemed so corny. If I was going to kill her, there was no need to drag it out by having her escape into the sewer.

I've heard it suggested that the reason Chet and Josie are together in hell at the end of *Ed the Happy Clown* is because that increases their punishment. Other people have suggested to me that it's a way of mitigating their punishment, that they really belonged together all along. Do you want to leave that choice to the readers or do you have a strong feeling one way or the other?

I should probably let people interpret it as they see fit, but I saw it as part of their punishment.

In issue #18, the whole issue is Ed, with no Matthew at all. In that issue we're told that Christian is "Agent Christian" and is from Mars. And we're also told that Ed gets disoriented if he's not wearing his clown make-up. I know that that material is left out, but I'm curious if either of those details should be seen as relevant to the finished book of Ed. Christian's a bit of a mystery. Should we see him as a Martian? And is what's said about Ed's makeup true for the rest of the text too, or should these things just be forgotten?

I'll leave those questions up to each reader.

On pages 11-12 of #18, the framing is different from anywhere else in the issue so far. Why?

Those weird panel borders were supposed to indicate that the sequence was a flashback.

The last panel of the *Yummy Fur* version of the Ed story in issue #18 depicts flames. At the time were you thinking of these as the fires of hell or simply Josie's burning house or both?

Yes, that's supposed to be the flames of hell at the end of YF 18.

In the "Fur Bag" section of #19, you say: "I only realized I was wrapping up the Ed saga while I was halfway through writing and drawing YF #17. (I think I was on page nine.) This would have been late June and the Ed book was too far into production to pull. Still we can always print a second Ed book reprinting 13-18 sometime or other. The orders for the book at hand, though, have been so ridiculously low that we're not anxious to rush into print with another one." To what degree did printing when you did, before it was over, fix the shape of the book? Do you ever regret not reissuing the Ed material that wasn't in the first Ed book?

I never regret not reprinting that material. Did printing the first edition of the Ed book when we did fix the shape of the book? I don't think I would have printed the YF-13-to-18 pages even if the first edition had been scheduled for later.

What was it like to shift gears in issue #19 once you were finished with Ed and move to writing more realistic pieces in which you yourself were often a character? Were you worried you might lose your audience?

I think I was both nervous about what the audience reaction would be and confident that I could make the autobiographical approach work.

Issue #20 has a meta-strip about writing "Helder," which is something you hadn't done before. Which was also different in that it wasn't paneled in the usual way. Did you feel like now that you were done with Ed you were getting a chance to try all sorts of new things?

Yes, it was very exciting to be working on the autobiographical stories after Ed.

In issue #23, the Playboy material has very different pagination than it does when it's collected as a book. How does that change it? Should one version be seen as definitive?

I wanted the artwork to be seen at a larger size. The definitive edition will be the one that's coming out in May [2013] (with all-new notes).

Can you talk a little bit about the shift to *Drawn & Quarterly* with issue #25? Did that have any effect on your production or your approach or focus or…?

Vortex publisher Bill Marks was never very fond of the autobiographical material, whereas D&Q's Chris Oliveros was enthusiastic about it. That was nice, but I'm not sure it affected the work in any way.

In the "Fur Bag" of Issue #25, you say "Keep your eye out for a book collection of my MARK adaptation to be published by Vortex later this year." Can you talk a little bit about why that didn't end up happening? Any plans to collect Mark and/or to finish Matthew?

Bill never paid me for the second edition of the Ed book, so I wasn't anxious to let him publish something else. There are no plans to reprint Mark or finish Matthew.

At this point would you be opposed to having Mark come out in book form because it's so different from what you're currently doing? Or would you not want to do it without the other gospels? Or has it simply not happened for various other reasons?

I'm reluctant to release it because it was poorly done.

In these later issues in the book of Matthew we start to have strange things happening. The demons driven into swine story, for instance, in #25—which is one of my favorite things you've done—is almost visceral, and it spills out to fill up the back cover as well. Also, we see Matthew picking his nose. Had your relationship to the material changed? You seem much more skeptical of the disciples here…

I always planned for Matthew to be more… visceral (for lack of a better word). And the **gospels** were skeptical about the disciples. But perhaps I did go too far in having Matthew pick his nose.

Can you talk about why you approached the demons driven into swine story in Matthew so differently from when you drew the same story in Mark? Is it more than just a difference in source?

I just figured it was going to be boring if I told the story the same way.

What made you decide to depict Ed's sister as a demon at the end of *Ed the Happy Clown* (202:6)? Was she always for you a demon?

To answer the second question first, no, I didn't always see her as a demon. It seemed like the right touch for that scene.

In issue #26, the Matthew story seems to be slowing down, covering only about a verse per page. By issue #27, we only cover a single verse in three pages. What was it about that material that made you want to spend more time with it?

It wasn't the material — I felt my approach for each of the gospels had to be different.

In the "Fur Bag" in #28, you talk about the "Definitive Ed Book" coming out, and say "Some of you may be wondering about issue 13 to 16 and 18. Well, I've decided I don't feel like reprinting the Ed Stuff in those issues and probably never will." Can you explain that decision?

Why not use the material from YF 13 to 18? Because it sucks.

You've mentioned that you don't intend to finish the Gospel of Matthew. Is this true? What made you decide to move on to other projects?

It's true. Other projects looked more interesting.

What about *Underwater*? What made you decide to not continue with that? Was it a question of sales or more that you lost interest in the story or…?

I had intended the series to be only twenty to thirty issues, but I didn't properly plan it out. At a certain point I realized that, to tell the story I originally wanted to, at the pace I had established in the early installments, 300 issues would be required. I didn't want to spend the rest of my life on the project. I should have written a script for the whole series before I began drawing it.

How hard do you find it to balance artistic and economic concerns (i.e. that you make your living selling comics)? Or is that generally not an issue?

Not that difficult. Most of my time is spent on my own projects. I only occasionally do I'm-only-doing-this-for-the-money jobs, and only if they pay really well. I don't get many of those sorts of offers, so I don't face temptation much. I wish I had more money, but most of us do. I've got enough for my basic needs, with some left over for fun.

Louis Riel was published in comic book form before it came out as a graphic novel. Did you find yourself changing much, if anything, in moving to the final book version?

For the book version, I redrew Riel in almost every panel for the first 79 pages. There were other minor changes.

Did you change anything for the ten-year anniversary edition of _Louis Riel_ or leave things pretty much as they were?

I corrected punctuation errors and rewrote a few sentences. The big addition is fifty pages of artwork that hasn't been widely seen, some of it hasn't been published before.

Plate 1. Cover of *Yummy Fur* #1

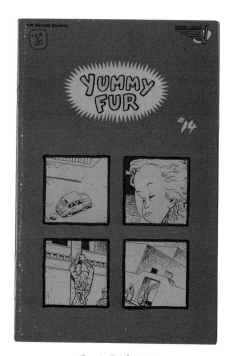

Comic-Book, 1986

Plate 2a. Various incarnations of *Yummy Fur* and *Ed The Happy Clown*

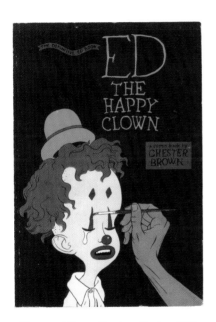

The second Vortex Comics collection, 1993

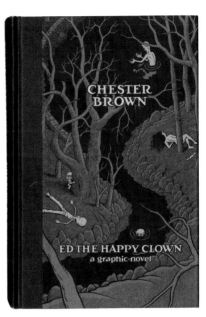

Drawn & Quarterly collection, 2012

Plate 2a continued

Drawn & Quarterly collection, 2012

Comic-Book, 1986

Mini Comic, 1983

Plate 2b. Various sizes of *Yummy Fur* and *Ed The Happy Clown*

Plate 3. Cover of *Yummy Fur* #5

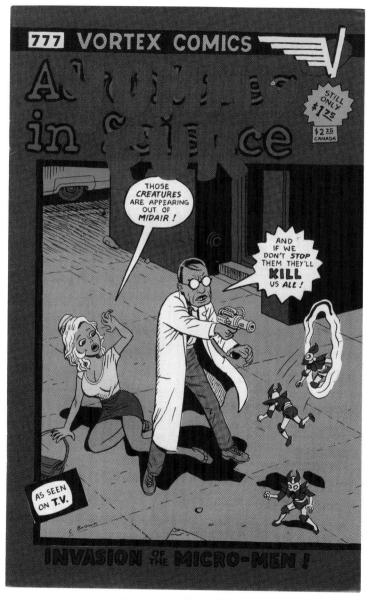

Plate 4. Cover of *Yummy Fur* #7

Plate 5. Cover of *Yummy Fur* #14

BRIAN EVENSON

Brian Evenson is the author of eleven prize-winning books of fiction. His work has been translated into over a dozen languages. He lives and works in Providence, Rhode Island, where he teaches at Brown University.

BOOKS BY BRIAN EVENSON:

Altmann's Tongue

The Din of Celestial Birds

Father of Lies

Contagion

Dark Property: An Affliction

The Wavering Knife

The Open Curtain

Last Days

Fugue State

Immobility

Windeye